Reading *and* Writing *in* Kindergarten

A PRACTICAL GUIDE

by Rosalie Franzese

SCHOLASTIC

PROFESSIONAL BOOKS

New York • Toronto • London • Auckland • Sydney
Mexico City • New Delhi • Hong Kong • Buenos Aires

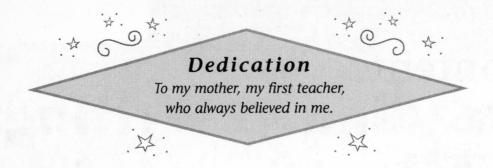

Dedication

To my mother, my first teacher,
who always believed in me.

I would like to thank Gloria Buckery, the exceptional Principal of P. S. 198 in New York City who supported my program and collaborated with me every step of the way, and MaryAnn Wainstock, a wonderful teacher and friend who was always so willing to learn and bring new ideas into her classroom. She never failed to provide me with the writing samples and photographs I needed to make this book come to life. Katherine Schneid and Emilia Macias are also two very dedicated kindergarten teachers who continue to bring the gift of literacy to children. I have had the pleasure of collaborating with Kelly DeGulis, Alison Wolensky, Tereasa Cavallo, and Tracy Markowitz, outstanding teachers who have also supported this program.

Maria Utevsky, my mentor from District Two, provided me with countless opportunities to grow through her inspiring support of my work. I am grateful to have her as a supportive learning force in my life. Elaine Fink and Anthony Alvarado were the first superintendents who recognized my work with the Distinguished Teacher Award, giving me the chance to begin this project. Bea Johnstone, Deputy Superintendent of District Two in New York City, is another important administrator who has always supported my goal of providing kindergartners with progressive literacy skills. Thank you to Hindy List for recommending me to Scholastic.

Thank you to my husband Steven for all the loving support he gave me during the many hours I spent on this project. My sister Marianne has given unconditional support, love, and belief in me from the day I was born. A special thank-you to my brother-in-law Lee. His comments and support were invaluable to me. Throughout my teaching career, my cousin MaryGrace has always helped me with her unique artistic talents. I will always cherish the loving encouragement I continue to receive from my mother and father. My brother Louis, sister Paula, nieces, nephews, aunts, uncles, and cousins have provided me with a lifetime of joy and inspiration. Thank you to Jenny Ruiz for your heartfelt administrative support.

Thank you to my editor, Jeanette Moss for all her hard work making this manuscript the best it could be. Thank you to Joanna Davis-Swing and Wendy Murray at Scholastic for all their efforts in bringing this project together.

Perhaps the most important, thank you to all the children who entered my classrooms and challenged me to create a program that could help them achieve their potential.

Finally, to all of my colleagues, supervisors, and distinguished leaders in this field, you have been exceptional teachers and have my great gratitude.

Cover photo and interior photos on pages 7, 15, 62, 90, 112, and 146 by James Levin.
All others courtesy of the author.

Illustrations by Rebecca Thornburgh

Edited by Jeanette Moss

Cover design by James Sarfati

Interior design by Sydney Wright

ISBN 0-439-22244-3
Copyright © 2002 by Rosalie Franzese
All rights reserved. Printed in the U.S.A.

2 3 4 5 6 7 8 9 10   40   08 07 06 05 04 03 02

Contents

Foreword

I have a passion for watching professionals performing their magic: be it the butcher trimming a pork loin, the orthodontist meticulously planning the curve of a wire, or the diver orchestrating the perfect performance, I am enthralled by the inherent beauty of the well-planned moves and flawless execution. Watching Rosalie Franzese work with a group of children, knowing each one's strengths and creating opportunities for them to be successful in their reading and writing, is a similarly moving experience. Rosalie is the consummate professional—passionate, knowledgeable, flexible, and relentless in the pursuit of her goals. And lucky us, in *Reading and Writing in Kindergarten: A Practical Guide*, she has taken the time to share with us her thinking and chronicle her practice in literacy teaching.

Rosalie Franzese has been a well-loved and highly respected classroom teacher, Reading Recovery teacher, and staff developer in New York City's District Two for more than ten years. This book centers on work she did over a two-year period when she pioneered the role of "distinguished teacher" at P.S. 198 in Manhattan in New York City. The distinguished teacher was to be a full-time coach and mentor to two classroom teachers, sharing in their planning and teaching, and ultimately sharing responsibility for the learning outcomes of the teachers and every child in their classes. Rosalie took on the mission with gusto, planning and revising planning daily, modeling and demonstrating, experiencing and revising techniques she had learned through her career, assessing and monitoring the children's progress, and working late into every evening preparing for the next day. The lessons she learned are available to us in this book. Rosalie walks us through the practical application of the theories behind the Balanced Literacy framework, detailing how she teaches each component of the framework and infuses it with the joy and sense of wonder that is every kindergartner's birthright. Readers will be impressed by the rigor of the work she describes; they will be equally impressed by the attention paid to creating an exciting and playful environment. At last, we have a description of rigorous teaching and dedication to the notion of sending every kindergartner to first grade reading and writing that will satisfy even the most ardent advocate of "developmentally appropriate" practice.

I was among those lucky enough to have witnessed Rosalie's work firsthand. I visited her at P.S. 198 dozens of times in those two years, armed with my home camcorder. I made amateurish videos to use in my teacher training sessions. Well, my videography may have been novice, but the teaching was so professional, and the children's work so compelling, that my teachers risked violent sea sickness as they watched the tapes to learn from Rosalie's practice. I am overjoyed that the publication of *Reading and Writing in Kindergarten: A Practical Guide* will enable thousands more teachers to witness, experience and learn from Rosalie's truly distinguished teaching. As you read it, you will realize that this is not one of those professional books that will spend its life on a shelf. This one is a keeper, folks. It will be one of your treasures—dog eared, underscored in multiple hues of highlighter, smudged from hundreds of handlings, always near the top of your pile of tried and true resources for planning. Read it, read it again, learn and enjoy!

—Maria Utevsky, Professional Literacy Consultant
for San Diego Unified School District

Introduction

This book is the result of the kindergarten literacy program that I developed and implemented in P.S. 198 in District 2, New York City. I drew upon my years of experience as a classroom teacher and reading specialist, as well as my years of training in Reading Recovery and the Arkansas method of teaching literacy. When I arrived at P.S. 198 as a Distinguished Teacher, the school was on the New York State Surr list, a categorization that threatens state takeover because the students' reading scores are well below the required state standards. Gloria Buckery, the principal of P.S. 198, was committed to having every child reading on level by the end of the second grade. Thus it was imperative that a revised literacy program be developed—one that would enable teachers to teach even the hardest-to-reach children successfully. This book presents the specific ideas, components and skills that I developed for the P.S. 198 Kindergarten Literacy Program.

I worked with kindergarten and first-grade teachers (in first-grade and kindergarten classrooms) to get the program up and running. The full support of our principal was a key to our success. Mrs. Buckery budgeted school funds and sacrificed a personal secretary to purchase needed books and materials. The teachers and I realized that if we were to succeed in having every child reading on level by the end of second grade, we had to start the program in kindergarten. It was with this sense of urgency that I entered the kindergarten classrooms of MaryAnn Wainstock, Katherine Schneid, and Emilia Macias, hardworking and dedicated teachers. We were determined to balance the accelerated instruction with a sense of play and student-initiated exploration

The traditional goals of kindergarten literacy are to make sure that students can write and recognize letters, begin to associate letters with sounds, and connect with literature in a more general way. When I began to think about the kindergarten program that I would create, I asked myself: *Can the students comfortably manage higher and more specific goals? Can I develop a curriculum in which the students will enjoy the process and enter first grade as competent readers and writers? And most important, can I make this a joyful experience for the children?* What happened during the following months was one of the most amazing experiences I've had as a teacher. The children were thrilled to learn to read and write. As their literacy skills grew, a hunger to learn more permeated the classroom.

P.S. 198 is now a model school in District 2. It is no longer on the Surr list, and the program I developed has been implemented throughout the primary grades. The children continue to flourish as readers and writers. The success I experienced at P.S. 198 is the result of a community of dedicated teachers working under the leadership of a principal with a vision and the strength to persevere. I am confident that the joy we experienced at P.S. 198 in not leaving any child behind on the road to literacy is within your reach. Hold onto the commitment and your vision will become a reality.

Chapter One

Getting Your Literacy Program Off to a Good Start

This book is designed to be a practical guide that will help a new or experienced teacher set up a comprehensive, effective literacy program in a kindergarten or primary-grade classroom. I want to help give teachers the confidence to prepare and put into practice a creative, playful, responsive, and meaningful literacy program for each child in their classrooms.

LITERACY IN KINDERGARTEN: A PLAYFUL, SUPPORTIVE ENCOUNTER

I've often been asked, "Isn't kindergarten the time when students should be immersed in play rather than instruction?" This question addresses the philosophical foundation of my literacy program. Play is essential in the lives of children.

It's how they make sense of their world. Play can be a lot of fun, but it's also serious work—challenging and full of opportunities for problem solving. Spontaneous, productive play can only happen in a context of trust, a place where a child feels free of judgment. What a child creates through playful activity is never wrong.

The spirit of play is at the heart of my literacy program. Children play with language, letters and words, and ideas to problem solve and and create meaning. The classroom is a playful arena of literacy in which kindergartners can realize their potential. They enter this arena without a history of academic failure. They enter with open hearts and minds. It is our primary goal as teachers to keep this spirit alive. There's no room for judgment. It's critical to honor and validate each child's personal response to the challenges of learning and to join in their delight at developing new skills. I'm convinced that every child can and will learn to read and write. I make sure to give each child the message every day in every encounter that he or she has what it takes to be a good learner. I let students know that together we'll figure out whatever we need to. This new arena of applied literacy, then, is at its essence playful and risk-free. The playfulness of the instruction isn't silly or unstructured; rather, it allows for satisfying and meaningful connections. As a result, children know that learning to read and write is exciting and fun.

THE KINDERGARTEN LEARNER

Kindergarteners enter your classroom eager to learn, and your role as guide to the world of literacy is vitally important. The children are like sponges, absorbing all they can. They can't wait to read the new Big Book or write a new story. I've found that kindergarteners can learn much more than has traditionally been expected of them. Beginning literacy instruction in kindergarten provides the children and the school with a significant advantage. The children go into the first grade with a firm grasp of early reading and writing strategies—a solid foundation on which to build.

THE PROGRAM

The structure of this book reflects the integration that is an important aspect of any successful literacy program. Each chapter explains a different component of the program. Yet each connects to and reinforces the ideas and skills presented in the others, and each of the basic components should be part of every kindergarten day. Here's an overview of the program and what each type of activity accomplishes.

❋ **Shared Reading** (The whole group reads enlarged pieces of text.)

◆ Provides a meaningful, whole-class reading experience.
◆ Teaches basic concepts about print.
◆ Models strategies and skills for independent reading.
◆ Promotes use of word-study skills.
◆ Introduces various genres.

❋ **Reading Play Stations** (Students work at purposeful and fun literacy activity centers.)

◆ Reinforce skills learned during Shared Reading.
◆ Introduce children to independent and partner work.
◆ Promote independent use of familiar strategies.
◆ Present skills in a fun and meaningful way.

❋ **Guided Reading** (Students at specific reading levels are taught in small groups.)

◆ Provides individual instruction at each child's level.
◆ Assesses skill levels.
◆ Informs lesson planning.
◆ Provides for individual prompting.

❋ **Read-Aloud** (The teacher reads different genres aloud to the whole class.)

◆ Lets children hear and enjoy literature above their reading levels.
◆ Models discussions about literature.
◆ Promotes responses to literature.
◆ Exposes children to new genres.

❋ **Independent Reading** (The children read on their own.)

◆ Promotes choice of reading materials.
◆ Provides the opportunity to apply learned strategies and skills independently.
◆ Assesses individual reading behaviors.
◆ Informs planning and instruction.

✦✦ Classroom Hint

Literacy Language for Kids

Translate literacy terms into child-friendly language. For example, in my classroom:

Quick-and-Easy Words = high frequency or sight words that children automatically know how to read and write from frequent encounters.

Chunking = The process in which a word's onset (the part of the word, or syllable, that comes before the vowel) is changed to form a new word with the rime, also known as the chunk (vowels and consonants that come after the onset). For example from *cat* can come *sat, mat, fat*, etc. In our class, we'd say, "What words can we get to from the word *cat*?"

Parts of Words = specific digraphs, blends, letter clusters, and endings, such as *-ing, -ed*, and *-s*.

Risk Taking (taker) = willingness to try out various strategies to figure out (solve) unknown words when reading and writing.

Power Name = students' names (one is selected each day) help children use their knowledge of—and interest in—their own names to learn about letters and words and solve new words.

Smooth Reading = reading naturally as we would when we're talking.

With their own language, your students will:

❋ have words they understand to refer to the processes involved in reading and writing.

❋ see how certain terms surface in all their literacy activities and be able to make connections.

❋ feel in control and thus gain confidence that they'll be able learn the skills they need.

❋ **Word Study** (The children make visual and meaningful sense of text.)

◆ Helps children understand how letters and words work.
◆ Provides ways to use word-solving strategies throughout the literacy program.
◆ Uses known information to build new knowledge.
◆ Integrates reading and writing instruction.

❋ **Shared and Interactive Writing** (As a class, teacher and students share in demonstrating the writing process.)

◆ Models early writing strategies.
◆ Introduces various materials for writing.
◆ Promotes creation and composition of meaningful text.
◆ Exposes children to different writing genres.

❋ **Independent Writing** (The children develop and write various texts on their own.)

◆ Models revision strategies
◆ Provides assessments that inform planning and instruction
◆ Supports the creation of meaningful text
◆ Provides experience with writing in different genres

Help Students Get the Connection

Keep pointing out to the children that skills they've already learned might apply when a new challenge arises. Model how they can solve almost any new challenge by referring to skills and strategies they've learned earlier. For example, during a Shared Reading lesson, I might highlight the chunk *et* in *wet* in a text we're reading and say, "It's like our quick-and-easy word *get*." I remind the children that when they're writing, they can use the chunk *et* to figure out and write new words like *let* and *set* that sound the same. I also ask the children to verbalize their thinking as they go through the process. This encourages children to analyze their thinking (be metacognitive) as well as get the idea that reading and writing are interrelated.

As you work with your students in the literacy program, you'll find that the skills and strategies the children learned for one kind of activity will surface in another. For example, the children will use a strategy taught in Shared Reading during an Independent Writing session. They'll use a skill learned during Guided Reading in an Interactive and Shared Writing experience. They'll use Word Study and problem-solving skills throughout.

SETTING UP THE ROOM

The way you arrange your room sets the tone for how you want your students to respond to the materials, the teacher, and each other. Your classroom will be the children's home and community for six hours a day, 180 days a year. You want to make it a stimulating and organized space they'll look forward to inhabiting.

Organize With a "Schedule-of-the-Day"

Setting out the daily events of your day can help you organize and pace your teaching. I write out a detailed schedule of the day for myself and post a simplified version for the children. I write each activity on a sentence strip and post it for the children to refer to. Next to each I place a photo of the children engaged in that activity, or I draw a picture that represents the activity.

My schedule might go something like this:

8:40–8:55	Unpack and sign-in
8:55–9:10	Morning Meeting—Morning Message, Power Name, Letter Strip
9:10–9:35	Song/Shared Reading
9:35–10:20	Guided Reading and Reading Stations
10:20–10:55	Word Study Activity/Class News using Interactive Writing with wipe-off boards
11:00–11:45	Lunch
11:50–12:10	Independent Reading
12:10–12:50	Independent Writing
12:50–1:30	Math
1:30–2:15	Prep (student attend specials, i.e. gym or music)
2:20–2:45	Read-Aloud

▲ *Our daily schedule in words and pictures, from Katherine Schneid's room*

❋ **Great places to learn.** The most important place in my classroom is a central meeting area where I do much of my teaching. I place a rug there, so all of the children can sit comfortably on the floor and easily see all the charts and books I teach with. Included in the area are:

◆ an easel for Big Books and chart tablets.
◆ individual wipe-off boards and dry-erase markers and space to store them.
◆ a large magnetic wipe-off board.
◆ a wall for the word wall, alphabet, and other word study charts.

I arrange the tables and chairs so that the children will be able to move around the room comfortably, and meet with partners and in small groups, depending on the activity.

❋ **Ways to celebrate children's work.** A kindergarten classroom should constantly reflect the children's current work and be full of all kinds of print, including the children's own words. Here are ways I display children's work:

◆ *Bulletin boards.* Throughout the year, I pin up children's new work or staple it to colorfully decorated bulletin boards. As lessons change—and the children provide more samples—I update and redecorate the bulletin boards (adding new borders can make this fun and easy). I title each board clearly and include a brief explanation of what is displayed.

◆ *Blackboard.* I display children's work and charts I used during instruction by quickly covering a section of the blackboard with colored paper.

◆ *Doors, closets, windows, and walls.* All available space can serve as colorful display areas.

◆ *Air space.* Hanging string from the lights and attaching papers with clothespins can be a beautiful way to display children's work.

◆ *All around the room.* Artistic displays around the room can help create a way to show off the children's work.

❋ **Super storage pulls it all together.** Organize your shelves, bookcases, and bins well, and you'll have come a long way toward making your literacy program run smoothly. If you plan your storage to make materials easily accessible and manageable for the children, you'll help your students become confident, independent learners. Try some of these ideas that have worked for me:

◆ *Store read-aloud books in the class library in small baskets and color code them.* Label the books according to author, topics, themes, or genre. I color

▲ *Labeled classroom library from Katherine Schneid's classroom*

code each book in a category with a sticky dot and put it in a similarly labeled basket. For example, I might have a basket labeled *Books by Eric Carle* and put a red dot on the label. I'd put all of Carle's books in the basket and attach a red dot to the corner of each one. With this coding system, children can learn how to put the books back where they found them.

♦ ***Keep Big Books used for Shared Reading lessons in the library area on specific shelves.*** There are also separate shelves used exclusively for Guided Reading and Independent Reading books. All the books are kept in baskets clearly labeled with the group's name.

♦ ***Establish a shelf space for each child.*** Each child's space is for materials to send home.

♦ ***Take advantage of tops of bookcases and shelves.*** These spaces can provide attractive ways to store poetry and writing journals for easy access.

♦ ***Give each Reading Play Station (see Chapter Three) its own basket or bin.*** Label each station and put it on a specific shelf (or shelves) labeled Reading Play Stations.

I spend several weeks at the beginning of the year modeling management of these literacy materials so that children can use them independently. The children learn, and the room stays organized.

What You'll Need for Kindergarten Literacy*

Shared Reading	Guided Reading	Independent Reading	Interactive and Shared Writing	Independent Writing
Big Books	Six copies of each text	Two-pocket folders	Chart tablets	Writing journals
Chart tablets	Baskets	Baskets	Blank Big Books	Various kinds of paper, including lined and blank
Songs, tapes, and cassette player	Two-pocket folders	Books at appropriate levels	Wipe-off boards/ dry-erase markers	Pens/markers
Highlighting tape/ wikki stix	Magnetic letters/ magnetic board		Markers	
Magnetic letters	Wipe-off boards/ markers for each child			
Magnetic board, wipe-off boards, dry-erase markers				
Correction and cover-up tape				

* See Chapter Three for a detailed description of materials needed for Reading Play Station activities

A Literacy Program Thinklist

- Set an exciting tone for learning and exhibit a love for learning.

- Let students know that you believe in them and have a vested interest in their success.

- Value and praise all student attempts.

- Establish a supportive environment where children can make mistakes without being judged.

- Tell all students that they are wonderful readers and writers. This makes it happen!

- Remind students that we can't waste our learning time.

- Instill the philosophy that we're a community of learners and that we learn from one another.

- Establish high expectations.

- Always focus on each child's strengths.

- Base teaching decisions and plans on the needs of the students.

- Plan every component of the literacy program carefully.

- Stress that all reading and writing skills are connected and interrelated.

- Encourage students to verbalize problem-solving strategies so they can internalize the processes.

- Always model and demonstrate what you want your students to do independently.

- Allow plenty of time for students to practice new skills and strategies.

- Set a quick pace.

- Keep the schedule structured and consistent.

- Be sure the children know exactly what to expect every day.

Chapter Two

Building Excitement with Shared Reading

Shared Reading, reading together as a whole group, is the starting point for your students' reading instruction. It should be part of every kindergarten day. (See pages 34 and 35 for sample weekly and yearly Shared Reading schedules.) It's a wonderful way to introduce children to unfamiliar texts and encourage their emerging excitement about literacy in a comfortable and supportive setting. Through Shared Reading, children internalize all the strategies and skills you model during the group demonstrations and transfer them to their own reading and writing.

THE BASIC SHARED READING LESSON

The children and I gather in our meeting area, and I place an enlarged piece of text on a book easel for everyone to see. In this setting, children can experience the

print, the illustrations, and the reading process as a whole. I begin the lesson by reading the text aloud. As students become familiar with it during a second reading (right after the first), they begin to participate by reading along with me. Using a variety of texts—Big Books, poems, and songs—for Shared Reading gives me the chance to model all the skills and strategies that students will need to become successful readers. I choose my text and a skill to focus on based on what my students need. (In later lessons, when children are more experienced, I include a variety of skills in one lesson.) In this non-threatening environment, every child can join in, even if he or she is unsure of certain words in the text. At first children need my support to read the selection independently. But as they become familiar with the text, my role diminishes, and they can read it on their own.

For each Shared Reading lesson I lead, I choose one familiar Big Book (the large text format, which was developed by Don Holdaway), so children can practice fluency and phrasing, and a new Big Book and poem to introduce words and strategies. Sometimes I may add another new Big Book if it reinforces the skill I am working on without overwhelming the class. The pacing during Shared Reading is critical. Don't spend more than twenty to twenty-five minutes on the entire lesson. And remember, your tone is as important as the strategies you're teaching.

USING BIG BOOKS DURING SHARED READING

When I introduce a new book, I first discuss the title and the pictures on the front and back cover, and I invite children to predict what the story might be about. For example, the cover of the Big Book, *Dinner!*, by Joy Cowley shows a chick eating a worm. I might refer to the title and illustration and say "Dinner? Do you eat worms for dinner?" Through their laughter, children will reply that the story is about a chick's dinner. Later I encourage my listeners to check if their predictions were correct by asking them to support their answers with evidence from the text. During the first reading, I use a pointer to model left-to-right direc-tionality and one-to-one spoken-to-printed word matches. On the second reading, children join in and read the text with me. At this point, they aren't reading each specific word. They're reading along as a group, saying the text from memory and using patterns such as rhymes and repetitive phrases, in addition to recognizing some specific words.

The main purpose of this first Shared Reading session with a new Big Book is for children to gain an understanding of what happened in the story. I want them

to understand that print carries meaning and that reading is a meaningful process. A sense of personal connection to the story being read helps with this understanding.

I ask children a variety of questions about the story and encourage comments and opinions based on their personal experiences. They respond orally, and then I ask them to find where in the book their observation occurred. A child will come up to the easel, turn to the specific page in the book that illustrates her comment, and read the text. Finally, I ask the child how she knew that was the correct page. She may respond by saying, "I looked at the picture," or "I looked at the word on the page." We go on to discuss the sequence of events and the various story elements, such as characters, setting, problem, and solution.

Favorites Big Books Through the Year

Beginning of the Year

The Birthday Cake by Joy Cowley (Wright Group)

I Am Eyes Ni Macho by Leila Ward (Scholastic)

The Long, Long Tail by Joy Cowley (Wright Group)

Who Lives in the Sea? by Sylvia M. James (Bookshop, Mondo Publishing)

Huggle's Breakfast by Joy Cowley (Wright Group)

Middle of the Year

I Went Walking by Sue Williams (Harcourt Brace)

Uncle Buncle's House by Joy Cowley (Wright Group)

Up a Tree by Joy Cowley (Wright Group)

What Comes First? (Bookshop, Mondo Publishing)

The Farm Concert by Joy Cowley (Wright Group)

End of the Year

The Cooking Pot by Joy Cowley (Wright Group)

Cookie's Week by Cindy Ward, illustrated by Tomie dePaola (Scholastic)

The Giant's Ice Cream by Jill Eggleton (Rigby)

Oh No! (Bookshop, Mondo Publishing)

The Jigaree by Joy Cowley (Wright Group)

To Town by Joy Cowley (Wright Group)

❋ Introducing a Big Book

Here's how I might introduce the Big Book *My Home* by Joy Cowley, which features the patterned text,"I like my home," said the ____. Each page shows a different animal's home, and the last page reads: *I like my home, said the space girl. My home can fly.*

The dialogue would go something like this:

Ms. Franzese: (Inquisitively to model phrasing and intonation) *What do you see on the front and back of this book?*

Children: *I see a snail, turtle, ladybug, and butterflies.*
I see a turtle.
I see a ladybug.
I see butterflies.

Ms. Franzese: (Show title page) *What do you see here?*

Christian: *A horse in a barn.*

Ms. Franzese: *The title of this book is* My Home. *What do the title and pictures make you think this story might be about?*

Emmy: *Maybe the animals are looking for a home.*
The book will tell us where the animals live.

Ms. Franzese: (Thoughtfully) *All of your predictions make sense. Let's read the book and find out.*

I read the book to the children.

Ms. Franzese: *What were some of the animals that liked their home? Susan?*

(Call on specific children. Throughout your lessons, encourage all children to volunteer.)

Susan: *Spider.*

Ms. Franzese: *Where does it say that in the book?*

Susan comes up and finds and reads the correct page.

Other questions I might ask my students include:

Why is the space girl's home special?

Why do you think the title of this story was My Home?

I want children to know that sometimes answers are stated in the text, but other times readers have to use their own thinking to grasp inferred concepts. The text implies that the space girl's home is special although it doesn't specifically state it. By reflecting on what they've learned from the text, children can infer that the space girl's home is special because it can fly and that the story is called *My Home* because it's about several animals' homes. By asking the questions and showing a sincere interest in their responses, I'm helping children learn to navigate text, encouraging their thoughtful reflection, reinforcing their comprehension, and validating their growing investment in learning to read.

✳ Promoting Fluency and Phrasing

As we reread familiar Big Books during Shared Reading, I continually model fluency, phrasing, and intonation. I tell the children that we're practicing <u>smooth reading</u>—to sound like we're talking. I teach them the meaning and use of a question mark, exclamation point, period, comma, quotation marks, and bold print. We find

---

Print Concepts to Point Out During Shared Reading

* Book cover: title, author, illustrator
* Title page: title, author, illustrator
* Where to begin: first page, first word
* Directionality: left to right, top to bottom, eye movement
* Left page precedes right page
* Return sweep: movement from one line of text to the next
* Difference between a letter and a word
* First and last letter of a word
* First and last word in a line of text
* Beginning and end of a sentence
* Number of sentences on a page
* Capital and lower-case letters
* One-to-one matching: spoken and written word

Adapted from *An Observation Survey of Early Literacy Achievement* by Marie Clay. (Heinemann, 1993).

• *punctuation marks*

18

these punctuation marks in the text and read the sentences together to create the phrasing and intonation that they indicate. When the children are comfortable with the feel and direction of the text as a meaningful whole, they're ready to focus on word-study skills. I place all the Big Books I've introduced through Shared Reading, in a specific area in the classroom library for students to reread during Reading Play Stations and Independent Reading.

❊ Teaching Word–Study Skills

I use the same Big Book the next day to introduce a word-study lesson, focusing on the visual sources of information within the text that will help students to figure out words (see Chapter Nine for details on word-study lessons). Word study is an integral part of any literacy program. Shared Reading lessons with Big Books are an important way to familiarize your students with some of the basic word-study strategies.

Quick-and-Easy Words. To teach a specific high-frequency word, a word students should learn to recognize and use automatically, I locate it in the story and put it on our Word Wall (see Chapter Nine). Children and I talk about how many letters are in the word and identify its first and last letter. As Patricia Cunningham suggests in her book *Phonics They Use* (2000), we chant the spelling of the word, clapping as we say each of its letters. The students and I call these words quick-and-easy words.

When students encounter a new text, they can automatically—and confidently—read the quick-and-easy words they've learned and focus their attention on new or more challenging text. From the beginning of the school year, children can learn approximately one to three new words a week. By the end of the year, they'll have learned approximately 100 quick-and-easy words.

Chunking: Onsets and Rimes. Once my students know the high-frequency word that I've taught, I go a step further. Let's say most of the class is confident in writing and reading the word *like* from the Joy Cowley's Big Book, *My Home*. I explain that sometimes if you know one word it can help you get to another word. As Margaret Moustafa has said, "The more print words children recognize, the easier it is for them to make analogies between familiar and unfamiliar words and to pronounce unfamiliar words" (1995). To model this concept (thinking aloud as I go along), I:

19

1. **form** the word *like* with magnetic letters;

2. **take away** the first part of the word (*onset*, any consonant that comes before the vowel in a word), in this case *l*;

3. **explain** that we're keeping the *chunk* (*rime*, the vowel and any consonants that come after the onset), in this case *ike*;

4. **put** another letter, *b* for example, in its place; and

5. **show** that we've made a new word, *bike*.

Then I ask someone to come up to the board and repeat the procedure with the word *like*. I use the term *chunk*, instead of *rime*, to avoid confusion with *rhyme*. To reinforce the strategy, I ask the child to say aloud what he's doing. He may respond, "I take away the first part of the word and put a *b* there and I keep the chunk *ike*. The new word is *bike*." As one child is forming the new word, I have another child write it on the wipe-off board.

I continue by asking the children, "How can I make the word *Mike*?" They tell me while showing me. When we've worked on a specific chunk, I write it on chart paper and post it as a reference so that when they're reading and writing, they can use what they know about one word to get to another.

❋ Teaching Reading Strategies by Masking Text

One day a week, using a familiar Big Book, I mask parts of the text by covering words or letters with removable tape. I may also mask words in the text by covering words or letters with tape and writing a different word on the tape. The new word may not sound right, have a reasonable meaning, or look right within the context of the text. In these cases, children can use what they've learned from previous Shared Reading lessons—about meaning, structure, and visual cues—to predict the words that are masked by the tape.

As we recap a masked-text lesson, the students and I identify and reflect on the strategies they used to predict text hidden by the tape. As we discover these things that "good readers do," we name them and add them to an ongoing class list; see sample chart at right. I write each strategy on a chart and

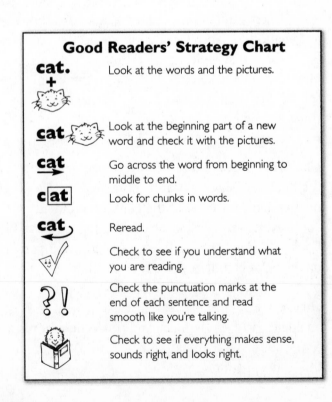

Good Readers' Strategy Chart

cat. + (cat image)	Look at the words and the pictures.
cat (cat image)	Look at the beginning part of a new word and check it with the pictures.
cat →	Go across the word from beginning to middle to end.
c‖at	Look for chunks in words.
cat ↵	Reread.
✓	Check to see if you understand what you are reading.
?!	Check the punctuation marks at the end of each sentence and read smooth like you're talking.
(person reading book)	Check to see if everything makes sense, sounds right, and looks right.

put an identifying picture icon beside it. I post the chart where all can see and make two smaller versions—one for children to use independently at school and one to send home to parents. I ask parents (through an explanatory letter) to use the chart to reinforce reading strategies at home, and I encourage children to refer to it at school when they come across a word they don't recognize. As the list of strategies grows, I make new copies for parents and children.

> **Good Readers' Strategies**
> *A reference chart for teachers*
>
> Good Readers:
>
> ❋ Use picture cues (illustrations in the book).
>
> ❋ Cross-check one cue against another: Look at the picture and the initial letter of the word.
>
> ❋ Reread.
>
> ❋ Think about what would make sense, sound right, and look right.
>
> ❋ Go across the word: Look at the beginning, middle, and ending.
>
> ❋ Look for parts of the word they may know (chunks *ook* in *book* or *th* in *thumb*).
>
> ❋ Self-Monitor: Notice errors.
>
> ❋ Self-Correct.

I reinforce the Good Reader strategies throughout the day during Independent Reading (see Chapter Six), when children read on their own, and Guided Reading (see Chapter Four), when children read in small groups. Children soon begin to transfer the knowledge from whole-class, Shared Reading lessons to their independent work.

At first, demonstrate only one strategy during masked-text lessons. (When children are more experienced, you can include several.) Choose the strategy based on what you've noticed your students need during independent or guided reading. For example, if you see that a student is skimming over the text too fast and missing words, you might focus on rereading for one-to-one matching. Or you may mask the text to illustrate cross-checking meaning and visual cues until you feel children have mastered that strategy. Throughout the year, you'll want to revisit and reinforce all the strategies you've introduced. Lots of practice not only reinforces skills and good reading habits, but it also helps children feel successful and ready to take on new challenges.

During a masked-text activity, I make sure the children verbalize the strategies they're using so that they internalize their skills and externalize their reasoning. For example, I may ask, "Why is that the right answer? How did you know that the other word wasn't correct?" Having to think through the process makes them aware they're using a strategy, one they can rely on again, especially during Independent Reading. After each masked-text lesson, we refer to our chart and discuss the specific strategies that we used to figure out the unknown words.

On the following pages are two examples of Shared Reading, masked-text lessons. The first is a beginning-of-the-year lesson using the book *Go, Go, GO* by June Melser. It focuses on one strategy: cross-checking meaning with visual cues. The second lesson comes later in the kindergarten year and uses the book *Along Comes Jake* by Joy Cowley. It demonstrates how I gradually move from focusing on one strategy to masking different aspects of a text to include a variety of strategies. After repeated modeling and application, children can figure out words they don't know by integrating the three cueing sources (meaning, structure, visual).

Beginning-of-the-Year Shared Reading, Masked-Tape Lesson

(Using the book *Go, Go, GO* by June Melser)

Text w/ Masking Directions	Strategy	Teacher	Children
I fly. Mask *ly* in *fly*.	Cross-checking one cue against another. (Students look at the picture (meaning cue) and the first letter of the word, *f* (visual cue).)	*What do you think the covered word is?*	**Cassandra:** Fly. *It says fly.*
Peel off tape.		*Let's check to see if you're right. Are you right?*	Yes.
		How did you know the word was fly? What did you do to figure it out?	*I looked at the picture and saw the dragonfly flying and I looked at the beginning of the word. It starts with f.*
		Terrific! That's what good readers do. They look at the pictures and the word.	
I swim. Cover the word *swim*. Write the word *run* on the tape.	Checking meaning cues.	*(As I read* run, *the students begin to laugh.)*	**Michael:** *That's not right. Fish don't run. They swim. The word should be swim.*
		Yes, run *doesn't make sense. What letter would you expect to see at the beginning of the word swim?*	**Jessica:** s.
		Let's see if you're right.	
Peel off beginning part of tape. The s shows.		*Are you right?*	Yes.
		What letter would you expect to see at the end of the word swim?	m.
Peel off all the tape to show the word.		*Were you right?*	Yes. Swim ends with an m.
		Good readers check to see if the word makes sense and looks right.	
I hop. Cover the word *hop* with tape. Write *jump* on the tape.	Cross-checking meaning and visual clues (initial and final letters).	I jump. *Does that make sense?*	**Sage:** Yes. Frogs jump.
Peel off the beginning part of the tape.		*What letter does this word start with?*	**Nina:** h
		So it can't be jump. What other word that starts with h would make sense?	**Gonzalo:** hop
		What letter would you expect to see at the end of the word hop?	p.
Uncover the word.		*Are you right?*	Yes.
		Great! Good readers check the beginning and end of the word.	

Later-in-the-Year Shared Reading, Masked-Tape Lesson
(Using the book *Along Comes Jake* by Joy Cowley)

Text w/ Masking Directions	Strategy	Teacher	Children
Ben helps Anne with the bed. Mask letter s in the word *helps*.	Checking if text sounds right and looks right.	Ben help Anne with the bed.	**Mark:** *That's not right.*
		Why, Mark?	*It doesn't sound right. It should be* helps.
		What letter would you expect to see at the end of the word helps?	*An s.*
Uncover the s.		*Are you right?*	*Yes.*
		(I reread sentence with students.)	**Louie:** *Now it sounds better.*
		Does it make sense?	**John:** *Yes. If you look at the picture, Ben is helping Anne fix the bed.*
		Good readers need to check that what they're reading makes sense and sounds right. It's also important to check the end of a word.	
Anne helps Dad with the garden. Mask the word *garden*.	Cross-check meaning with structure.	Anne helps Dad with . . . *What word would make sense and sound right?*	**Destiny:** *Garden. They're in a garden.*
	Read across the word.	*What would you expect to see at the beginning of the word* garden?	**Danny:** *g.*
Peel off tape to show g.		*Are you right?*	**Danny:** *Yes.*
		What would you expect to see in the middle of the word garden?	**Carl:** *ar like in* car *and like in my name Carl.*
		What chunk is at the end of the word garden?	**Nina:** *en like in* then.
Peel off tape to show entire word.		*Is the word* garden?	**Paige:** *Yes.*
And then along comes Jake. Mask the capital A with a lower case *a*.	Check beginning of sentence for capital letters.	*Does everything look right?*	**Ricky:** *No. The* a *needs to be a capital.*
		Why?	*Because it's the beginning of a sentence.*
(Peel off tape to check.)		*Are you right?*	*Yes.*

Text w/ Masking Directions	Strategy	Teacher	Children
Mom helps Dad with the car. Cover the word *with*.	Recognize high-frequency words.	*What word is missing?.*	**Jose:** *With.* (Child writes *with* on wipe-off board.)
Peel off the tape.		*Are you right? Check with word in the book.*	*Yes. I'm right.*
Anne helps Mom with the bathroom. Cover the word *bathroom*.	Integrate meaning, structure, and visual cues.	*What are some words that might make sense and sound right in this sentence?*	**Children:** *Toilet, cleaning, bathroom.*
	(Write the children's words on the board and say them slowly.)	*Let's check to see which word looks right.*	**Children:** (They compare words to see which is like the word in the text.) *Bathroom,* they all say.
Mom helps Ben with the bike. Cover the word *bike* with the word *truck*.	Cross-check meaning with visual information.	*Is there anything wrong with this sentence?*	**Jennifer:** *Yes. There's no truck in the picture. There is a bike. The word should be bike.*
	Look for chunks.	*What other word do you know that can help you get to the word bike?*	**Andrew:** *Like. If you know like, you can get to bike. It has the same chunk.*
		Show us.	(Andrew writes *like* on the board.) *If you take away the l and put a b and keep the chunk ike, the new word is bike.*
		Check to see if you're right.	(Andrew peels off the tape and checks the text.)
And then along comes Jake! Mask the exclamation mark with a question mark.	Check the punctuation marks.	*Then along comes Jake?* (I read with questioning intonation.)	**Michael:** *That's not right. It's not a question. Everyone's mad that Jake is coming because he messes everything up.*
		What mark should be at the end of the sentence?	**Jasmine:** *An exclamation point.*
		Why?	**Louie:** *They're upset that he's coming.*
		Let's check. Louie, will you write an exclamation point on the board and then check under the tape?	(Louie writes an exclamation mark and checks under the tape.)
		Good readers look at the end of each sentence to check the punctuation marks. Then they know if they should read in a questioning or excited voice or just stop.	

24

✾ Thinking Aloud to Build Confidence

Frequently when I read a Big Book aloud to children, I think out loud about how I'm trying to figure out a word. By modeling my thinking process, I'm showing children that it's okay to feel confused or unsure when they are presented with new material. Say I'm trying to figure out the word *cow*. My soliloquy might go something like this:

> **Humm, I'm not sure what this word is . . .**

Then I look at the pictures and say aloud what the children might be thinking about what's happening in the story.

> **I wonder what word would make sense here . . .? Could it be cow, horse, bull, duck? The picture does have a lot of animals in it. Now let me check to see what the word looks like. Do I know any parts or chunks in this word? Or another word that can help me get to this word? It begins with a c. Oh, I see the chunk ow, like in Howie's name. I think the word is cow.**

At this point I continue:

> **Now, I'll go back to the beginning of the sentence and see if this word sounds right, looks right, and makes sense. (Read sentence with the word "cow.") What's happening in the story? Yes, the story is happening on a farm. I think cow makes sense.**

This reinforces the idea that reading is meaningful, and that it's important for children to understand what they're reading.

At the end of this activity, I always have children reflect on what they observed, and, referring to our Good Readers' Strategy Chart (see page 20), we discuss the strategies they noticed me using. After I've demonstrated this type of strategy building many times, I have children do their own problem-solving out loud using an unfamiliar Big Book. I explain that good readers try to figure things out on their own and are not afraid to be risk-takers even though they may make mistakes.

Children won't be willing to risk making a mistake unless you create a nurturing, non-threatening environment. One way I do this is to promote the idea of taking chances and making an effort. I ask the children excitedly, "Who wants to be a risk-taker?" Because of my tone and my validation of risk-taking, the children are eager to volunteer. I call one child up to try to read a page from the book on his own. If he gets stuck on a word, the group uses the Good Readers' Strategy Chart to make helpful suggestions. For example, a child may suggest, "Look at the picture and look at the way the word begins!" If a reader makes a self-correction, I ask him to verbalize his thought process for the rest of the

group. Children love this approach, and it helps them become cooperative problem-solvers as well as independent readers and writers.

✸ Big Book Lessons to Encourage Writing

After a beginning-of-the-year Big-Book, Shared Reading lesson, I have children respond by writing their own versions of the text; we call these writings *innovations*. Innovative writing with Shared Reading instruction helps build the reading-writing connection. Just as children learn to stretch and pull pieces of text apart to create meaning when reading, you can show them how to mirror the process by having them put text together to create new meaning through writing. Children use the repetitive pattern or theme of the Big Book to create their own versions of the story or text. Having children write innovations supports reading and writing skills.

Modeling Big Book theme-and-pattern writing. Here's an example of how I may model innovative writing after reading a Big Book. The book is *In the Mirror* by Joy Cowley, and the text reads:

> *See my fingers.*
> *See my toes.*
> *See my tongue.*
> *See my nose.*
> *See my elbow.*
> *See my knee.*
> *See a monster—that's me.*

1. I ask, "What do you see when you look in the mirror?" Through Shared Writing strategies, (see Chapter Seven), I model a response by answering and writing *See my nose.* I write it on the easel, using the same paper that the children will use when they write independently. As I write, I demonstrate what I want them to do when they write. For example, before writing the word *See,* I say "I'm going to make a capital *S* because *See* is the beginning word of my sentence." I explain that *see* and *my* are quick-and-easy words, so I write them without hesitation. As I write the word *nose,* I stretch out the word slowly and record the letters of all of the sounds that I hear. I explain that you need a silent *e* at the end of the word *nose* to make it look right.

2. I give each student a piece of paper that has three separate lines on it. It looks like this: _____ _____ _____. *See my nose.*

Sometimes I may have already written one of the words from the repetitive phrase to focus the children on the unwritten part. As the year progresses, I

find that I don't need to provide the lines anymore.

3. I draw a picture to match the text and emphasize that good readers use pictures to help them figure out unknown words.

4. In preparation for writing on their own, I have children discuss with a partner what they're going to write. And I have them tell me what they are going to write. As I repeat what each child says, I point to the lines on the paper to show that they will write one word on each line. This also demonstrates one-to-one matching of spoken words to written text.

5. Children go to their seats to write on their own. They write the words *see* and *my* and then the new or innovative word. They may use invented spelling for the new word. I support students who need extra assistance by writing letters and words that they're unable to make on their own.

6. Each child contributes a page, which I staple together with the other pages to form a child-created Big Book.

Throughout the week, we continue to work on learning the high-frequency words *see* and *my* from the lesson. At the beginning of the year, I model and write the letters or words for children who are unable to write them. Later they can do it themselves.

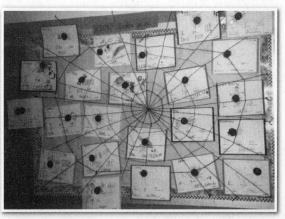

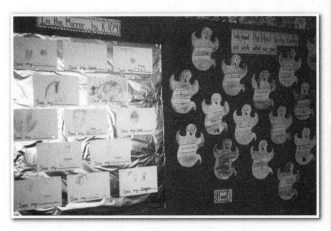

Children use the repetitive pattern or theme of a Big Book to create their own versions, or "innovations," of the story or text. These displays are from Katherine Schneid's kindergarten classroom.

Displaying students' innovations. I display students' work in a variety of ways depending on the overall theme of the Big Book. For example, when I posted the classes' versions of *In the Mirror*, I made a big mirror out of aluminum foil, glued each child's story to it, and hung it up. Let's say the Big Book shows animals going down a hill; you might draw a big hill and post children's stories at different levels on the hill.

When the children's work is on display, I write the correct spelling of an invented-spelling word on a small yellow sticky note and place it underneath their word. One of the purposes of this writing activity is to teach children high-frequency words within context. As more and more innovations are put on display, your classroom fills up with print that children can read independently.

Turn Innovative Writing into Class-Connected Big Books

Besides creating versions of Big Books you're reading in Shared Reading, you might base class books on themes or holidays. Include pictures and photographs. These texts, which are so familiar to the children, are great for reading practice. Rereading them helps the children develop fluency and phrasing, as well as reinforce reading strategies. As you take the children's innovations off the walls to make room for new ones, make them into books for the class library.

Here are some ideas for class Big Book:

✴ ***Use photographs of children participating in regular classroom activities*** with captions underneath such as *John is reading.*

✴ ***Create a book of the children's favorite riddles***—riddles for Shared Reading lessons or riddles children write themselves. Note: Riddle books are great for practice with such high-frequency words as *it, is, in, on.* Underneath each riddle question, write the answer and cover it with a sticky note. Let children peek under the sticky notes to check their answers. For example: *It is red. It is a fruit. It is round. What is it?* The word *apple* would be written under the riddle and covered with a sticky note. Take past written riddles and make a book out of them. The children can use the same structure to write their own riddles.

✴ ***Make a feeling book*** by taking pictures of the children making different facial expressions, or having the children draw pictures of different facial expressions. Captions for the pictures could be *I am happy (sad, angry, frustrated, scared)* or you can use the child's name and write *Jane is happy.*

❋ Using Nonfiction Big Books

Besides storybooks, we read a variety of nonfiction Big Books during Shared Reading. We discuss and compare the different features of fiction and nonfiction. Students learn that fiction books are stories about make-believe people and places, whereas nonfiction books tell about real people, places, and things. Children also learn to identify and understand the following characteristics of nonfiction books:

- ✓ Photographs with captions
- ✓ Diagrams with labels
- ✓ Headings
- ✓ Table of contents
- ✓ Index

USING POEMS DURING SHARED READING

I read at least one poem in addition to a Big Book with every Shared Reading lesson. I choose, or create, poems that reflect the word-study skills we're working on and that correspond with the structure or patterns found in the Big Book. For example, when we read the Big Book *My Home*, and children were learning the word *like*, I wrote a poem that includes the word *like* as well as words with the *ike* chunk in them:

> *I like to ride my bike.*
> *I like to go on a hike.*
> *I go with my friend Mike.*

I also include other poems that have the word *like*, but don't have rhyming words with the same chunk.

At the beginning of the year, I introduce familiar nursery rhymes and coordinate movements with the words to provide rhythms and patterns that will help children connect to the text. For example, if the line of the poem reads, "Humpty Dumpty had a great fall," we roll our hands to accompany that line. The movement makes the lesson more fun and helps children remember the line.

❋ Poems Enhance Word-Study Skills

Because many poems and nursery rhymes are already familiar to the children, they're particularly effective for introducing word-study skills such as *chunking* and locating *quick-and-easy words*. After reading a nursery rhyme or poem that rhymes, I ask children, "What words sound the same?" This helps children understand that most words that sound the same have the same *chunk (rime)*. For example *spoon* and *moon* from the nursery rhyme "Hey-Diddle-Diddle" sound the same because they have the *oon* chunk.

Have your students identify words that look and sound alike or are quick-and-easy words they already know, such as *the*, *see*, and *go*, by covering them with highlighting tape. At the beginning of the year, I include lots and lots of familiar nursery rhymes and chants to teach the concept of chunking. I want them to *hear* which words sound the same before I point out—and they see—the letters and chunks that are the same. We chart words with matching chunks and display them near our Word Wall (see Chapter Nine). For example, during a Shared Reading lesson, we may read the nursery rhyme "Rain, Rain Go Away."

> *Rain, rain go away.*
> *Come again another day.*
> *Little children want to play.*
> *Rain, rain go away.*

I invite someone to come up and highlight all of the words that sound the same. We notice that *away*, *day*, and *play* sound the same because they have the same chunk (rime) *ay*. After the children have mastered the word *day*, we construct new words (perhaps *say*, *may*, *ray*, and *today*) from the *ay* chunk. This is excellent practice for problem solving to learn new words.

I often send home the poem that the children are working on as a homework activity. I ask children to circle, underline, or fill in any deleted high-frequency words or chunks that we're working on; see the sample homework page below.

One way for children to learn high-frequency words and chunks within context is to have them frame the words in the poem by placing one finger at the beginning of the word and the other finger at the end of it. We also use highlighting tape and wikki stix to frame words. Sometimes as I'm reading the poem, I delete rhyming words, and children tell me what's missing. I have them check to see if their response looks like the word in the poem.

❈ Poetry Journals

Each child keeps a poetry journal comprised of a three ring binder and the poems we've worked on during Shared Reading. Each Friday, I have students put a copy of the poem we read that week in their journals. Children take their journals home once a week and read the poems to their families. The poems on page 31 can be used to promote the use of chunking.

Name _____

Fill in the missing words from the poem, "I Love To…".

I Love To…

I love to _____to the beach.

I love _____ play in the sun.

_____ love to splash in the water.

I _____ having fun!

_____

| I | go | love | to |

The Moon

Why does the moon
go big and small?
Why doesn't it stay
like a big silver ball?

I Wrote a Story

I wrote a story.
I made a book.
I wrote a story,
Come and look!

Little Bird

Little bird,
Little bird
Why can't you fly?
I can, I can
If I try, try, try!

—three by Jill Eggleton

Sally Go Round the Sun

Sally go round the sun,
Sally go round the moon,
Sally go round the chimney tops
On a Saturday afternoon.

Cleano

We wash our hands
With a rub rub rub
We take a bath
With a scrub scrub scrub
We take a swim
With a glub glub glub
Rub Rub Rub
Scrub Scrub Scrub
Glub Glub Glub
Cleano Cleano
Rub Scrub Glub

—by Sonja Dunn

I love to . . .

I love to go to the beach.
I love to play in the sun.
I love to splash in the water.
I love having fun!

—Jill Eggleton

I use poems from a variety of sources and also make up my own poems using familiar, high-frequency words or the new word that I'm working on that particular week. One good source for poems is *101 Thematic Poems for Emergent Readers* published by Scholastic. During the planning sessions with the kindergarten teachers I worked with, we wrote the poems on page 32 to promote high-frequency words:

I Go . . .
I go to the pool.
I go to the school.
I go up the tree
To see a bee.

Where Are You?
He is at school.
She is at the pool.
They are at the park
And will come home when it is dark.

What Is It?
A book?
No, No, No!
A cat?
No, No, No!
A bat?
No, No, No!
A boy?
Yes, Yes, Yes!

I Go, Go, Go
I go up the ladder.
I go down the slide.
I go up the hill.
I go up.
I go down.

I See
I see the car.
I see the train.
I see the bus.
I see the plane.

I Am
I am so glad.
I am so sad.
I am so mad.
I am me!

I Read With . . .
I read with my mother.
I read with my dad.
I read with my teacher.
I read when I am glad.
I read, read, read!

Love, Love, Love
He loves me.
Love, love, love
She loves me.
Love, love, love.
I love me.
Love, love, love.

We wrote the following poems to take advantage of using familiar names. For the children's names, each day we put a sticky note with a different child's name on the blank line.

Where is _____? (child's name)
Here I am!
Where is _____? (child's name)
Here I am!
Where is _____? (child's name)
Here I am!
We are all at school!

Where is _____? (teacher's name)
Is she in the library?
No!
Is she at home?
No!
Is she at the park?
No!
Is she in school?
Yes!

USING SONGS DURING SHARED READING

The children and I sing a song in the morning, or I find 10 or 15 minutes each day to sing. I write the songs on chart paper with pictures that match the words. I point to the words as children sing along to reinforce directionality and the concept that the spoken word matches the written text. We make up movements to go with the words. The children love to sing and move. The familiar rhythms and different sensory patterns help them to connect the song they're singing with the printed text.

Singing is a good way for children to practice locating known words or letters within context. Sometimes I ask children to locate or frame a particular word, or I locate the word and ask them to tell me what it is. After we collect several songs, I make individual songbooks by attaching the songs with paper fasteners and putting them inside a manila folder labeled "Class Songbook." I keep adding new songs to the folder. Once a week the children take home their songbooks and practice singing the songs with family and friends.

Good Sources for Songs

Be flexible. You can use any song by any artist that you think the children may enjoy. Here are two songs and some books I like to use:

Alligators All Around. This tape of the Maurice Sendak book, sung by Carole King, is a wonderful song for illustrating letter-sound correspondence and developing fluency and phrasing.

Today is Monday by Eric Carle, published by Scholastic, is a fun song to teach your children.

The ABC Sing-Along Flip Chart and Tape, also from Scholastic, includes a collection of simple, catchy songs for each letter of the alphabet— another great way to introduce letter-sound correspondence within a meaningful context.

The Songs and Rhymes Teacher's Book: Stage 1 from Mondo is a good resource.

Scholastic's Teaching Tunes series by Dr. Jean Feldman is another good source for songs.

Here's how I might combine songs and Shared Reading in my lesson plan for the week.

Sample Weekly Shared Reading and Song Schedule

Monday:	• Song to review quick-and-easy words (same song all week) • Introduce and read new Big Book for the week • Introduce and read new poem
Tuesday:	• Song • Reread this week's Big Book: word-study lesson introducing one quick-and-easy word • Reread Monday's poem to introduce quick-and-easy word
Wednesday:	• Song • Reread this week's Big Book for a word-study lesson on chunking onsets and rimes and to reinforce the quick-and-easy word • Reread poem • Read new poem to introduce a second quick-and-easy word
Thursday:	• Song • Mask text in this week's Big Book and poem for meaning, structure, and visual cues • (Read a second new Big Book to reinforce strategies and word study skills we've been working on if students are ready for it.) • Reread poem—practice forming, writing, and locating second quick-and-easy word
Friday:	• Song • Reread this week's Big Book for phrasing and fluency, locating new words and chunks • (Reread second new Big Book for phrasing and fluency, if applicable.) • Reread poems—frame quick-and-easy words

Shared Reading Instruction—Year at a Glance

	Beginning of the Year September–December	**Middle of the Year** December–March	**End of the Year** March–June

A blue cake.

A pink cake.

A pink cake.

Up in a tree,
what do I see?
I see a bird,
and it sees me.

"What have you got
for dinner, Mrs. Spot?
What have you got
in your cooking pot?
Is it cold?
Is it hot?
Will we like it, Mrs. Spot?"

Text Characteristics to Teach

Beginning of the Year

from *The Birthday Cake* by Joy Cowley

- Two words or one to two sentences per page
- Repetitive patterns with a simple storyline
- Pictures strongly support text
- Similar high-frequency words repeated throughout text
- Print and illustrations placed consistently
- Definite spacing between words
- Punctuation marks (period, exclamation point, question mark)

Middle of the Year

from *Up in a Tree* by Joy Cowley

- Two to six lines of print per page
- Patterns and repetition in some books
- Stories a bit more complex but still understandable/predictable
- Pictures still supportive but focus is more on print.
- Range of high-frequency words increases
- Full range of punctuation marks
- Word endings such as *ing*, *ed*, and *s*

End of the Year

from *The Cooking Pot* by Joy Cowley

- Three to eight lines of text per page
- Stories are more complex (definite beginning, middle, and end)
- More characters introduced
- Placement of text and illustrations varies
- Illustrations still support the story, but text is more important
- Variety of high-frequency words used
- Varied word endings and longer words
- Occasional repetition of phrases
- Range of punctuation, especially dialogue

Skills and Knowledge to Model

Beginning of the Year

- Front/back of the book
- Left page precedes right page
- Title page, author, illustrator
- One-to-one matching
- Directionality
- Difference between a letter and a word
- Identify first and last letter of a word
- Use pictures to figure out unknown words
- Begin to cross-check meaning and visual cues (initial letter of word)
- Make predictions based on title/cover
- Make predictions based on pictures
- Locate known words in a line of text
- Begin to learn high-frequency words
- Identify words that sound the same
- Chunking (using a known word to form a new word)
- Begin to focus on fluency and phrasing
- Make personal connections

Middle of the Year

- Directionality
- Return sweep
- One-to-one matching (Does spoken word match written word?)
- Cross-check meaning and structural cues with visual cues (beginning, middle and ending of a word)
- Notice chunks (*ook, ike*) and parts of words (*sh, th, wh, ch*)
- Read and locate a variety of high-frequency words
- Use known information about one word to form a new word
- Reread
- Self-Monitor (checking to see text makes sense, sounds right, looks right)
- Discuss meaning and use of punctuation marks (period, exclamation point, comma, quotation marks)
- Develop fluency and phrasing
- Discuss aspects of story (who, what, where, when, why, how)
- Sequence events in story
- Confirm and reassess predictions

End of the Year

- Integrate meaning, structural, and visual cues
- Reread
- Self-monitor and self-correct
- Look for known parts and chunks within words
- Reading and writing a variety of high-frequency words
- Fluency and phrasing
- Locate evidence within story to support answers to questions
- Make inferences
- Discuss components of story (character, setting, plot)

Chapter Three

Reinforcing Skills at Reading Play Stations

Reading Play Stations (literacy activity centers) engage children in playful, fun, game-like activities. But this kind of meaningful and purposeful play, which comes out of Shared Reading, Word Study, and Interactive Writing lessons (see Chapter Seven), gives children practice with the skills they're learning and provides the support they need to become independent readers. Each station includes one focused activity that may have one or more steps. I introduce the stations and model their use in September (about six weeks before we begin Guided Reading groups). Then, when I begin meeting with separate Guided Reading groups (see Chapter Four), the other children work at the stations independently or in groups of two or three. By then they're already familiar with how the stations work and need little assistance. At any one time, I may have as many as eight stations available. Children simply gather the necessary materials, group their chairs together, or find places on the carpet to work together at the stations. Children love the play stations; they're learning to work together, and they're learning in a fun way.

INTRODUCING READING PLAY STATIONS

Reading play stations require a great deal of whole-class modeling before children can use them independently. It's important to introduce them gradually—one or two at a time—so children aren't overwhelmed. We begin by discussing the stations in general—what they should look like and how important it is to use "inside" voices when working at them since many children will be doing a variety of activities at the same time. I demonstrate every station activity to the whole class at the same time. I also have some children model how to play a station game while the others look on. Then we all discuss their observations. After some stations are up and running, and during the first six weeks of school before Guided Reading begins, I walk around and monitor children as they work in the stations. After station time, we always discuss the positive things that happened as well as what we still need to work on.

MANAGING READING PLAY STATIONS

❋ Charting the Course—Station to Station

Before we begin working in the stations, I develop a Reading Play Station Schedule Chart that shows students what stations they'll be working on. There are lots of ways to set up a reading station chart (see photos on page 38). Just be sure your system is simple and clear so children are confident as they move around the room from station to station.

One of my station charts uses a "house" theme and is color-coded. For each group of five or six children, I make a different colored house. I attach the names of the children in a specific group to the roof of a house with velcro®. The composition of station groups matches that of the Guided Reading groups, once they are established. I can assign each child a partner by placing the two names side by side on the house. I also make station icons, on which I write the name of the station and draw a picture of the station. I put three of these inside the house below the names, with the first icon corresponding to the first pair of children, the second icon to the second pair, and so on. I decide which students will go to what stations based on their individual needs. Once the children have finished their initial assigned station, they can go to any of the other two stations in their house, if the other children have finished working in them.

Another way to set up a station chart is to use a pocket chart. Put the station icons on the left side of the chart and two children's names to the right. The children find their names on the chart and go to the stations indicated by the icon.

There are lots of ways to set up Reading Station Charts.

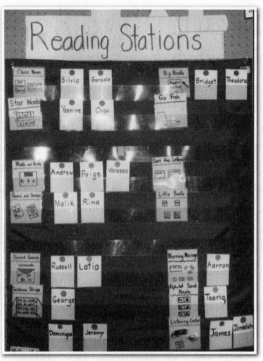

MaryAnn Wainstock's Reading Station Chart.

❋ Station Materials

Each station has its own bin, basket, or plastic bag labeled with the same icon used for the reading play station chart. I keep all the stations in a specific area in the classroom where children have easy access to them. Many of the stations require magnetic letters and boards and plastic sorting trays. You'll need several sets of upper- and lower-case letters and some sorting trays, each of which contains separate compartments. It's important to store the letters—with several of the same letter (mixing upper and lower case) in each compartment—so the children don't have to spend time searching for letters.

Magnetic letters and boards, sorting trays, and wipe-off boards are available through Steps To Literacy LLC (www.stepstoliteracy.com) or Lakeshore (www.lakeshorelearning.com) catalogues. Other materials frequently used in reading stations, such as index cards, dry erase markers, letter picture cards, alphabet charts, and baggies can be purchased at any office supply, stationery, or teacher supply store.

❋ Making Changes

I continually update the play stations and develop new activities as the need arises. Every week I make minor adjustments, such as incorporating information from a new Big Book, new high-frequency words, or new messages into the structure of existing stations. If children don't need practice with a specific skill anymore, I take away the station that reinforces it. Every four to six weeks, I take stock of the stations, and if I notice that students need more help with mastering a specific skill, I create a new station for it. I make sure to send children to the specific stations that meet their individual needs.

SAMPLE READING PLAY STATIONS

❄ Name Games

We use name-game stations primarily at the beginning of the school year. Most children enter school able to recognize and write some aspect of their names. Knowing their own names gives them a sense of identity, and this familiarity with their names and the letters in them provides a powerful way for you to introduce word-study skills. In addition, familiarity with classmates' names reinforces early reading and writing skills while building a sense of community. We make the children familiar with all of the students' names by working with a different "power name" during our daily class meeting (see details on page 150 in Chapter Nine).

Classroom Hint

Give the Answers and See Them Learn

Answers are provided on an answer key in many of the Reading Play Station reading activities. Don't worry that some children may just *copy* the provided *answer*. Generally they won't. They enjoy the challenge of trying something out and then checking to see if they're right. But when a child gets really stuck, she can look at the answer key for support. This is an important and acceptable way for children to learn—especially at the kindergarten stage of development.

Here are some activities to use with names in a reading station:

Make My Name

To use at the beginning of the year

▲ Materials/preparation:
Magnetic letters in a sorting tray, magnetic board, wipe-off boards, index cards
Make name cards for each child.

▲ Skills practiced:
Quick-and-easy word recognition; letter and word formation; letter-sound correspondence

▲ What the children do:
1. Make their names with magnetic letters from the sorting tray on a magnetic board.

2. Look at their name card and check to see if they formed their name correctly.

3. Practice writing their name on a wipe-off board using their name card as a model.

▲ Variations:
◆ Write each child's name on an index card, laminate it, and cut the letters apart. Put the letter cards and a name card in a plastic bag—one for each child. The child lines up the letter cards to make her name and checks it

against the name card. The child also finds the names of the other children in the class and forms them.

- Using interlocking cubes, take out as many cubes as there are letters in the child's name and put a sticky dot on each cube. Write one letter of the child's name on each sticky dot. Put each set of cubes in a plastic bag. The child puts his name's letters in the correct order.

- Have children make their classmates' names as well as their own.

- On every name card, highlight or underline certain parts of each name. For example, in *Jonathan* underline the *th* so students to learn the digraph sound of *th*. Only highlight parts that have already been introduced to the class during the daily power-name activity (see Chapter Nine).

Say My Name (and Match the Sound)

To use at the beginning of the year

▲ **Materials/preparation:**
Make a set of class names and a separate set of picture cards, each representing a letter of the alphabet. You can make picture cards from index cards and pictures found in magazines, old unusable books, alphabet poster charts, and alphabet matching games.

▲ **Skills practiced:**
Letter-sound correspondence; cross-checking meaning with visual cues; quick-and-easy word recognition

▲ **What the children do:**
1. Place the set of class names on the table.
2. Choose a picture card and match it to an appropriate name card. (For example, if a child picks up a picture of a kite, she may place it next to the name Kenny.)
3. Match other picture cards and name cards.

Clap My Name

To use at the beginning of the year

▲ **Materials/preparation:**
Make a set of laminated name cards and three separate "beat" cards—one reads 1, another reads 2, and another reads 3.

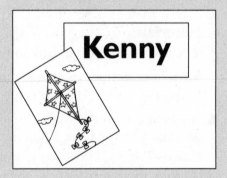

Teacher Tip

As part of a daily activity, I have the children recite an alphabet chart (*Aa apple, Bb ball*) during the class morning meeting. At the beginning of the year, I copy the pictures on that chart and put them on cards for match-ups in the name-game station. Once the children master those letter-sound correspondences, I make new pictures so they can apply their knowledge to new information.

Kenny

▲ **Skills practiced:**

Separating words into syllables

▲ **What the children do:**

1. Spread out the beat cards on the table.

2. Choose a name card, read it, and clap the number of syllables in the name. (For example, the name *Mary* would have two claps.)

3. Place the name card under the appropriate beat card—one for *Sam*, two for *Mary*, three for *Felicia*.

4. Repeat with other name cards.

5. Have partners check their layouts.

✽ **ABC Station Games**

I introduce ABC stations at the beginning of the school year and generally remove them by December. They promote familiarity and fluency with the alphabet, letter identification, sound correspondence, and letter formation.

Sorting Letters ⋯⋯⋯⋯⋯⋯⋯⋯⋯⋯⋯⋯⋯⋯⋯⋯⋯⋯

To use at the beginning of the year

▲ **Materials/preparation:**

Magnetic letters (a mixture of upper- and lower-case letters stored in a bin), two cookie sheets or two pieces of laminated cardboard—one surface labeled capital letters and one labeled lower-case letters

▲ **Skills practiced:**

Distinguishing between upper- and lower-case letters

▲ **What the children do:**

1. Choose a letter, say its name, and place it on the capital or lower-case surface.

2. Have partners check their work.

Sticks, Dots, Circles and Tunnels ⋯⋯⋯⋯⋯⋯⋯⋯⋯⋯⋯⋯⋯

▲ **Materials/preparation:**

Magnetic letters sorted in a sorting tray according to the lesson

Label four sections of a large piece of construction paper *Letters with Sticks, Letters with Dots, Letters with Circles, Letters with Tunnels.* Under each label draw a circle big enough for magnetic letters. Write letters within the circles, depending on what you want the children to work on. For example, under *Letters with Sticks*—T, E, F; *Letters with Circles*—p, d, q; *Letters with tunnels*—h, m n. Remind children to refer to upper-case and lower-case letters on the alphabet charts.

▲ **Skills practiced:**

Distinguishing distinct features of the letters of the alphabet

▲ **What the children do:**

1. Match the letters in the circles with the magnetic letters in the sorting tray.

2. Have a partner check them.

▲ **Variation, more advanced:**

Make separate, laminated cards for each feature with picture shapes, but no letters written as models. For example, the *Letters with Circles* card has a circle on it but no letters. I make new cards with added features such as *sticks and slants—k* and *z*—and *circles and sticks—b* and *a*. Print the correct letters on the back of each card. The children place the letters that fit the heading on the card. To check their work, they slide their letters off the card and look at the back.

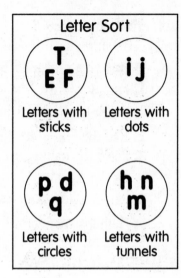

Letter Sort

Letters with sticks — T E F

Letters with dots — i j

Letters with circles — p d q

Letters with tunnels — h n m

Letter Shapes ....

To use at the beginning of the year

▲ **Materials/preparation:**

Cardboard, yarn

On separate pieces of cardboard draw and cut out following shapes: a slanted line, a tunnel, a hook, a straight line, a circle, a curved line, and a straight and slanted line together. Punch holes in the cardboard pieces; see sample of curve and straight line art at right.

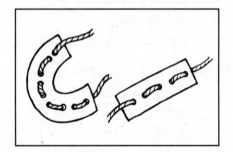

▲ **Skills practiced:**

Distinguishing shapes that make up letters; developing motor skills for writing

▲ **What the children do:**

1. Pull the yarn through the holes.

Children can do this activity before they actually sort the letters according to shapes.

Letter Making ....

To use at the beginning of the year

▲ **Materials/preparation:**

Cardboard, glue, buttons or beans

On separate pieces of cardboard, draw each letter of the alphabet and outline them in block style; use numbers and arrows to show how the letters are formed.

▲ **Skills practiced:**

Letter formation; motor skills used for writing

▲ **What the children do:**

1. Glue beans, buttons, or Cheerios® within the outline of each block letter.

2. Use the arrows and numbers as a guide for forming the letters in writing.

3. Run their finger over the beans, buttons, or Cheerios and verbalize the movements they're making to form the letter. For example, for the capital *L*, they would say "down, across."

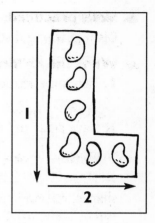

Missing Letter Game

▲ **Materials/preparation:**

Index cards, magnetic letters in a sorting tray, wipe-off boards, copies of alphabet charts

Make three sets of cards. One set leaves out the initial letter in a series of three alphabet letters (_, B, C; _, e, f). One leaves out the middle letter (A_C; d_f). One leaves out the final letter (G, H _; j, k _). Write the missing letter on the back of each card.

▲ **Skills practiced:**

Fluency with alphabet sequence

▲ **What the children do (in pairs or individually):**

1. Read the card and figure out what letter is missing.

2. Choose the correct letter from the sorting tray.

3. Write the letter on a separate wipe-off board.

4. Check their work by turning over each card and looking at the correct letter on the back.

Letter Strips

To use at the beginning of the year

▲ **Materials/preparation:**

Magnetic letters in a sorting tray

On a paper strip, write a series of letters in both upper and lower case, out of sequence.

▲ **Skills practiced:**

Fluent recognition and identification of letters; recognition of similar attributes among letters

▲ What the children do:

1. Place a magnetic letter from the sorting tray on top of the matching written letter on the strip of letters.

2. Take off each matched letter and say its name.

▲ Variation, more advanced:

On large laminated cards, draw two circles and in each of the circles write letters that have similar visual features—three of the same and one different. Write the answers on the back. In one circle, you might write the letters *v, w, v, v,* and in the other the letters *p, p, q, p.* The children place the correct magnetic letter on top of each written letter and then select the one letter in each circle that is different. Then, they turn the card over and check their work.

Stamping Out Letters

To use at the beginning of the year

▲ Materials/preparation:

Two sets of upper- and lower-case letter stamps and pads—one for each partner
On one sheet of paper write all the capital letters of the alphabet with a line next to each. Do the same with lower-case letters.

▲ Skills practiced:

Matching upper- and lower-case letters

▲ What the children do:

1. On the capital-letter sheet, stamp the correct matching lower-case letter.

2. On the lower-case sheet, stamp the correct capital letter.

Letter Bingo

To use at the beginning of the year

▲ Materials/preparation:

Cardboard for bingo cards and letter cards, bingo markers
Divide pieces of cardboard into six to eight sections, and write a capital letter in each box. Make separate letter cards for each capital letter of the alphabet.

▲ Skills practiced:

Recognition of upper- and lower-case letters

▲ What the children do (groups of 3):

1. One child calls the letter while the others children see if they have that letter on their card. If they do, they place a marker on that letter.

2. All players fill up their cards to finish playing the game.

▲ Variations:

- Make a bingo game with lower-case letters.

- Once the children have mastered upper- and lower-case letters, make a game with a combination of upper- and lower-case letters.

- Towards the end of the year, make a picture-bingo game with blends (when two letters combine and each sound can still be heard, as in *tr* or *bl*) and digraphs (when two letters combine to make one sound, as in *sh* and *th*). For example, on a bingo card divided into six sections, write a blend or digraph in each section. Each child gets a different playing card with different blends or digraphs. I prepare a variety of playing cards with a picture on the front and the word for the object along with the matching letter combination written on the back. The children choose a card, say the name of the picture, figure out what blend or digraph it begins with, and place a marker on that letter combination on the bingo card. For example, if they choose a picture of a *shoe*, they would say *shoe*, place a marker on *sh*, and check the back of their card to confirm.

ABC Charts

To use at the beginning of the year

▲ Materials/preparation:
Pointer, variety of alphabet charts

▲ Skills practiced:
Letter-sound correspondence; fluent recognition of letters

▲ What the children do:
1. Choose an alphabet chart; point to and read the letters on it. (For example, students would read the chart as described in *Apprenticeship in Literacy* by Dorn, French & Jones (1998) as follows: *A, a apple, B, b ball, C, c cat.*)

2. Choose other charts to read from. (This helps the children understand that the letter *A* in one chart is the same as the letter *a* in another chart. It shows them that knowledge is stable. They also begin to realize that *ball* and *bike* can begin with *B* or *b*.)

I Begin With . . .

▲ Materials/preparation:
Velcro®, cardboard

Draw and cut out shapes of familiar objects such as a door, a heart, and so on. Draw a speech bubble for each shape, laminate each, and stick pieces of Velcro® on the backs of the pairs. On each speech bubble write the phrase *I begin with* and the letter and name of one of the cut-out objects. For example, for the cut

out of a door, the matching bubble would read *"I begin with D," said the door.* Make a cut-out object for each letter of the alphabet.

▲ Skills practiced:
Letter-sound correspondence; one-to-one matching; punctuation

▲ What the children do:
1. Read the words on each laminated, cut-out speech bubble and use the Velcro® to match it with the appropriate object.

▲ Variation, advanced:
Once the children have mastered the letters of the alphabet, make shapes that represent blends and digraphs. For instance, cut out a question-mark shape and make a speech bubble that says, *I begin with* qu, *said the question mark,* or cut out a tree and make a bubble that says *I begin with* tr, *said the tree.*

| Letter Books | ···

To use at the beginning and middle of the year

▲ Materials/preparation:
Staple together little four- to five-page books made of typing paper

▲ Skills practiced:
Letter formation; understanding context and meaning making; letter-sound correspondence and formation

▲ What the children do:
1. Choose a letter of the alphabet to write on each page. Children draw a picture of something that begins with the letter's sound on each page.

2. Label the pictures by articulating the word slowly and writing the sounds that they hear.

3. Write the letter on the front cover.

| Sound-O | ·····························

To use at the beginning and middle of the year

▲ Materials/preparation:
Cardboard, pictures from magazines, old posters, and unusable books with initial sounds for each alphabet letter
Divide a cardboard game board into 26 sections and write a different letter of the alphabet on each. Also prepare 26 picture cards (each show-

A student plays Sound-O.

46

ing an item beginning with a different letter). Write the name of the object on the back of its card and underline its initial letter. For example, if the card has a picture of a dog on it, write the word *dog* on the back and underline the letter *d*.

▲ Skills practiced:
Letter-sound correspondence

▲ What the children do:
1. Pick up a picture card, say the name of the object aloud, and place it on the letter that corresponds to the initial sound of the object.

2. Continue until all the letters on the game board are covered.

3. Remove the cards, checking each one against the word on the back.

Picture-Sound Match

To use at the beginning and middle of the year

▲ Materials/preparation:
Cardboard, pictures to represent the sounds of the initial alphabet letters
Divide a piece of cardboard or heavy paper into six sections. Draw or cut out three pictures and glue them on the top three sections of the card. On the bottom three sections write (in random order) the letters that correspond to the pictures above. Laminate the card.

▲ Skills practiced:
Letter-sound correspondence

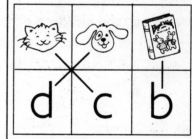

▲ What the children do:
1. Match the pictures to their appropriate initial letters by using an erasable marker to draw connecting lines.

▲ Variation:
Set the game up so that the pictures represent ending consonant sounds, or digraphs (*sh, th, wh, ch*), or blends (*br, bl, sw*).

Puzzle Pieces
To use at the beginning of the year

▲ Materials/preparation:
Index cards
Cut each index card in the shape of two puzzle pieces. On one piece write the capital letter and on the other write the lower-case letter.
Note: Don't put out all of the letters of the alphabet at the beginning of the school year. It's too overwhelming for the students. Put out six or seven letter sets and separate them into different plastic bags—for example, *A-G* in one plastic bag and *H-L* in another.

▲ **Skills practiced:**

Identifying and matching upper- and lower-case letters; reinforcing knowing letter names

▲ **What the children do:**

1. State the name of each letter as they match them.

▲ **Variation:**

Make matching letter and picture (initial letter of object matches letter sound) puzzle pieces. At the beginning of the year, reproduce the pictures from the alphabet chart used for demonstrating letter-sound correspondence. For example, *Pp* would go with a picture of a pencil.

| Transparency Letters | .... |

To use at the beginning of the year

▲ **Materials/preparation:**

Index cards, transparency sheet, dry-erase marker

Write each letter of the alphabet on a card. On each, draw arrows and numbers to assist with forming letters. (See example on page 43.)

▲ **Skills practiced:**

Letter formation

▲ **What the children do:**

1. Trace over the letters with the marker and verbalize the movements. (For example, if a child were forming the letter *L*, she would say *"down and across."* The numbers show which line to draw first, and the arrows indicate the direction.)

▲ **Variation:**

Children practice forming letters in a sand or salt tray.

✺ **Word-Study Reading Stations**

Introduce word-study reading stations throughout the school year. Those used early in the year may focus on learning and practicing skills using one word, while stations introduced later in the year may apply the same skill within a larger context. Each station builds on skills the children learned at previous stations and prepares them for new skills. Word-study stations reinforce quick-and-easy words, chunking skills, and aspects of word formation.

| Word Bingo | .... |

▲ **Materials/preparation:**

Construction paper or cardboard, bingo markers—you can make square markers

out of colored construction paper or use any other appropriate material.

Create game boards by dividing two or three pieces of paper into six to nine boxes. Write the words you're currently working on—one in each box—in different order on each card. Each card includes a word or two that is different from those on the other cards. On each of separate cards, write one of the words from the game boards.

▲ Skills practiced:

Reading and identifying quick-and-easy words

▲ What the children (two or three) do:

1. Each child gets one bingo card and bingo markers.

2. One child holds up a word card.

3. The children read the word and see if they have that word on their bingo card. If they do, they place a marker on the word.

Students play Word Bingo.

4. When someone fills up his or her entire card, a new game begins.

You should update this station on an ongoing basis, adding and deleting words according to the words you're working on at the time.

Making and Breaking

To use throughout the year

▲ Materials/preparation:

Magnetic letters in a sorting tray

In a plastic bag, place word cards containing new words from the Word Wall. Put the magnetic letters in a sorting tray with a separate compartment for each letter so the children don't have to spend time searching for letters.

▲ Skills practiced:

Reading and forming quick-and-easy words

▲ What the children do:

1. Take one word card out of the plastic bag and read it.

2. Form the word using the magnetic letters.

3. Read the word again, running their finger underneath it, checking to see if it looks right.

Look-Say-Name-Cover-Write-Check

(From a technique developed by Diane Snowball, *Spelling K–8: Planning and Teaching*, (1999)
To use in the middle of the year

▲ Materials/preparation:

Index cards, library pocket cards, cardboard, wipe-off boards
Prepare one index card for each high-frequency word the children have learned.
On library pocket cards—one for each letter of the alphabet—write a lower- and upper-case letter. Glue the pocket cards to separate pieces of cardboard—eight to a piece. Put the words in the appropriate pocket (*go* in the *G, g* pocket for example). This is a great system for organizing the high-frequency word cards.

▲ Skills practiced:

Reading and writing quick-and-easy words

▲ What the children do:

1. Take one word card from a pocket, look at it, read it, name the letters of the word.

2. Turn the card over so the word is covered; then write it on a wipe-off board.

3. Turn the card back to show the word and check it against what they wrote.

▲ Variation:

Have the children clap and chant as they name each letter.

Word Shape-Up Game

To use throughout the year

▲ Materials/preparation:

Cardboard, Velcro®
Write high-frequency words on cardboard and cut out their shapes. For example, the shape around the word *the* would include a taller side to fit the *t* and *h*, and then drop down to fit the *e*. The bottom part would be a straight line since there are no letters such as *g* that would cause the shape to drop down to fit the hook of the *g*. Then, outline the shape of each letter on another piece of cardboard and cut it out. You'll have shapes with words on them and shapes that are blank; see sample at right. Put Velcro® on the back of the word shape and on the front of the blank shape.

▲ Skills practiced:

Distinguishing and matching features and configurations of letters and words

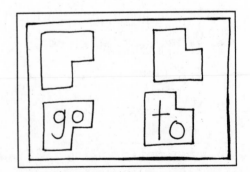

Template for Word Shape-Up Game

▲ What the children do:

1. Fit the word in the correct shape.

Let's Go Fishing

To use throughout the year

▲ Materials/preparation:

Cardboard, magnetic tape, bowl, unsharpened pencil, a piece of string, a paper clip, magnetic letters in a sorting tray
Cut out 10 to 15 cardboard fish and write one high-frequency word on each. Stick a piece of magnetic tape on each. Put the "fish" in the bowl. To make a fishing rod, tie a large paper clip to the end of the string and attach the string to the end of the pencil.

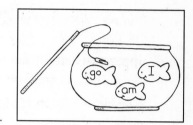

▲ Skills practiced:

Reading, forming, and writing quick-and-easy words

▲ What the children do:

1. One partner puts the fishing rod in the bowl, picks up a fish and reads the word on it.

2. The other partner makes the word with magnetic letters.

3. Each of the partners keeps a written list on a separate sheet of paper of all the words they caught.

Word Concentration

To use throughout the year

▲ Materials/preparation:

Cardboard
Make two sets of identical word cards.

▲ Skills practiced:

Quick-and-easy word recognition (similar to the game Memory®)

▲ What the children do:

1. Place the word cards face down.

2. Take turns flipping over two cards.

3. Read the words that they turn over and see if they have a match. (If they do, they remove those cards.)

Once all of the matches have been made the game is over.

Rhyming and Chunking

For the beginning of the year

▲ Materials/preparation:

Index cards

Create up to seven sets of cards—one picture card (a picture on the front and the word for it with a chunk highlighted on the back) and another picture card with a different picture and word but the same chunk.

▲ Skills practiced:

Understanding the concept that words that rhyme or sound the same usually have the same chunks in them

▲ What the children do:

1. Spread out the cards with the pictures face up.

2. Pick up a picture card (e.g. a picture of a *boat*) and say the word.

3. Find the picture card with a matching chunk *oat* (e.g. *goat*) and say that word.

4. Turn over both cards and check to see if the chunks match.

Flip Books

Flip books for the ook chunk.

To use in the middle of the year

▲ Materials/preparation:

Index cards, hole punch, binder rings

On the right hand side on an index card, write a chunk you're working on. Punch a hole in the top center of the left hand side where the chunk is *not* written. Cut several other index cards apart, sized so that when you write a letter or two on them and line them up with the chunk, they will form a word. Punch holes in the top center of the smaller pieces and put a binder ring through all the holes (the one on the left side of the chunk card and the ones on smaller cards) to form a flip book. See illustration at right.

▲ Skills practiced:

Chunking to use information from a known word to make a new word; understanding that putting different letters in front of the same chunk makes new words

▲ What the children do:

1. Use the flip book to make different words and read each word. (If the chunk on the index card is *ook*, for example, they flip the attached letter cards to see letters they can combine it with to make new words, including *l* for *look* or *sh* for *shook*.)

2. Make each word with magnetic letters.

Let's Highlight!

To use at the end of the year

▲ **Materials/preparation:**

Cardboard, pictures, highlighting tape
Make two sets of picture cards—one for beginning sounds
and one for ending sounds—and write the word for each
object on the backs of the cards (you'll use these sets
separately). Highlight the beginning or ending sound.
Under or next to each picture, list three choices of beginnings or endings of words. For example, if the card has a
picture of a zipper on it and you're teaching ending
sounds, the choices might be: *ed, er,* and *ing.* On the back
of the card, the word *zipper* is written and *er* is underlined.

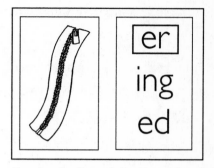

*Template for front of picture card for
"Let's Highlight"; on the back, the word
zipper is printed with the* er *highlighted.*

▲ **Skills practiced:**

Identifying, articulating, and isolating beginnings and endings of words

▲ **What the children do:**

1. Say the name of the picture slowly and listen for the ending or beginning
   sound.

2. Place a piece of highlighting tape over the correct choice. (They can use the
   same piece of tape for the entire activity.)

3. Turn the card over to check their answer, where the name of the object is
   written and the correct beginning or ending sound is underlined.

Word Sorting

To use in the middle of the year

▲ **Materials/preparation:**

Index cards, magnetic tape, magnetic board
Write one word on each of four or five index cards
and place a piece of magnetic tape on the back of
each card. Choose words that contain specific
chunks that you're working on with the class.
Include words with two different chunks.

Teacher Tip

As the children begin to master the
concept, include three categories.
Here's an example: The words to sort
are *like, look, cat, Mike, hike, shook, took,
bike, hook, hat, cook, spike.* The children
sort the words according to the
chunks *ike, ook,* and *at.*

▲ **Skills practiced:**

Recognizing and sorting visual attributes of letters and words to enable
new-word formation during reading and writing

▲ **What the children do:**

1. Categorize or sort the words on a magnetic board or the side of a file cabinet
   according to their chunks.

Missing-Word Bingo

For the end of the year

▲ **Materials/preparation (three children):**

Posterboard/cardboard

Divide sheets of cardboard into six boxes. In each box write a sentence leaving out a quick-and-easy word. Replace it with a line. Prepare word cards for each of the missing words.

▲ **Skills practiced:**

Integrating meaning, structure, and visual cues

▲ **What the children do:**

1. One child picks up a word card and reads the word.

2. The other players read through the sentences on their boards to see if they have the sentence that the word fits into; the word has to make sense, look right, and sound right.

3. Once a child completes his or her card, the children choose another card and repeat the activity.

Roll the Chunk

To use at the end of the year

▲ **Materials/preparation:**

Two cubes or dice, dry-erase markers, magnetic letters in a plastic bag

Place a sticky dot on each side of two cubes or dice. On one of the cubes, write the chunk you're teaching on each sticky dot on all sides of the cube. On the other cube, write on each sticky dot a different letter or letter combination that will form a word with the chunk. (For example, if the chunk is *ook*, the letters might be *b* for *book*, *l* for *look*, *c* for *cook*, or *sh* for *shook*.) For each set of cubes, prepare a sheet of paper listing sentences with a word missing. Write the chunk that the sentences correspond to on the bottom corner of the paper. Put a picture cue next to each sentence.

Laminate each sheet. Place sets of cubes in plastic bags. Prepare an answer sheet for each set.

▲ **Skills practiced:**

Chunking and forming new words from familiar words; integrating meaning, structure, and visual cues

▲ **What the children do (partners take turns):**

1. Throw the two cubes or dice and read the word that the cubes make.

Teacher Tip

You may have four different chunks using eight different cubes at this station at one time. However, keep each set of cubes separate from the others so that the children work with one set at a time.

54

2. Use the magnetic letters to make the word.

3. Read the sentences and look for the one sentence that fits the word.

4. Check to see if the word makes sense in the sentence using meaning, visual, and structural cueing.

5. Write the missing word on the laminated sentence sheet with a dry-erase pen.

6. The other partner repeats the sequence.

7. When the sheet is filled, the partners check it against the answer sheet and erase the words before going on the next set.

I like to <u>LOOK</u> at birds.
I love to read a <u>BOOK</u> in school.
I <u>TOOK</u> my sister's toy.
I put my coat on the <u>HOOK</u>.
The leaves <u>SHOOK</u> on the trees.
I like to <u>COOK</u> soup.

Name _____ Jane _____
Rhyme Time
"Little Bird" by Jill Eggleton
Little bird,
Little bird,
Little bird,
Why can't you fly?
I can, I can
If I try, try, try!

Rhyme Time

To use in the middle and end of the year

▲ **Materials/preparation:**
Highlighters
Make multiple copies of a rhyming poem that you've read during Shared Reading. Place them in a basket along with highlighting markers.

▲ **Skills practiced:**
Chunking to use information from a known word to make and write a new word

▲ **What the children do:**
 1. Read a copy of the poem.
 2. Highlight all of the words that sound the same.

Filling in the Missing Chunk

For the end of the year using more challenging text

▲ **Materials/preparation:**
Dry-erase markers
Write a passage from a familiar Big Book or poem on a piece of paper, leaving out words with similar chunks. Laminate the sheet.

Teacher Tip

Make sure to select poems that contain rhyming words that look the same (have the same chunk). The children should fully understand that if they know one word it can help them to get to another word. Many words sound the same but do look different. If children notice this, acknowledge their observation, but don't do a formal study of it in kindergarten. Wait until first grade to study this more advanced concept.

▲ **Skills practiced:**

Using chunks as a visual cue; cross-checking for meaning, structure, and visual cues

▲ **What the children do:**

1. Fill in the missing word with a dry erase marker.

2. Read the poem to see if it makes sense.

3. Erase their work so the next child is able to use the laminated sheet.

By coming up with the missing words *get* and *wet* on their own in this poem, the children understand that knowing the word *let* will help them form *get* and *wet*. The cross-checking skill acquired in this chunking activity, which is practiced within a meaningful context (a whole poem, song, or passage), rather than in isolation, helps children figure out words during independent reading.

> Name _____ Tom
>
> **"Grandpa, Grandpa"**
> by Joy Cowley.
> Grandpa, Grandpa.
> Come with me.
> Let us go fishing
> In the sea.
> What did we fish for?
> What did we <u>get</u>?
> We got <u>wet</u>!

from Grandpa, Grandpa by Joy Cowley. Copyright (c) 1980 by Joy Cowley. Illustrations copyright (c) 1980 by David Cowe. Reprinted by permission of The Wright Group, 19201 120th Avenue NE, Bothell, WA 98011-9512.1-800-523-2371.

| **What's the Word** | · |

For the end of the year (requires a more sophisticated use of the chunking process and that children be able to read unfamiliar sentences independently). This is not introduced as a station until this word-study activity is practiced with the class.

▲ **Materials/preparation:**

Index cards, dry-erase markers

Make laminated task cards, each giving a written clue for a specific word on the Word Wall, where quick-and-easy words are displayed in alphabetical order. For the word *get*, for instance, one card may say, *It starts like* goat *and rhymes with* wet. Other examples: *It starts like* ladder *and rhymes with* bike (*like*), or *It starts like* thumb *and rhymes with* when (*then*). (You may want to draw pictures next to the content words such as *ladder, goat,* and *bike.*) Number each card and put it and a numbered-to-match answer card in a plastic bag.

▲ **Skills practiced:**

Using onsets and chunks to form new words

▲ **What the children do:**

1. Choose a card and find the correct word on the Word Wall.

2. Write the word on the card.

3. Check their work with the answer sheet and erase it when finished.

❋ **Whole-Context Reading Stations**

The following stations give children the chance to integrate and apply skills

they've learned during literacy instruction. They involve the various texts and materials—Big Books, poems, songs, morning messages and class news—students have been exposed to every day in the classroom.

Big Book Buddy Reading ····················

To use throughout the year

▲ **Materials/preparation:**
A set of Big Books that you've worked on as a class

▲ **Skills practiced:**
Fluency and phrasing; one-to-one matching; cooperative learning

▲ **What the children do:**
1. Partners read familiar Big Books and help each other figure out any unknown words by using reading strategies they've learned during the Shared and Guided Reading lessons.

2. Read in unison or take turns reading alternate pages.

3. Use a pointer to point to each word read.

Buddy reading of familiar Big Books

Poetry Strips ····················

To use throughout the year

▲ **Materials/preparation:**
Large business-size envelopes
Write each of the poems you've read during Shared Reading on the outside of an envelope. Also write each poem on sentence strips, one line to a strip of paper, and put these in the envelope. Draw a picture clue beside each line of the poem on both the outside of the envelope and on each sentence strip.

▲ **Skills practiced:**
Sequencing for meaning; cross-checking meaning with visual cues; practicing quick-and-easy words

Practicing reading strategies with poetry strips

▲ What the children do:

1. Read the poem.

2. Remake the poem with the sentence strips.

Variation:

You can make this station more challenging by cutting the sentence strips into words.

Guess and Check ·······························

To use throughout the year

▲ Materials/preparation:

Magnetic tape, plastic bags, cardboard
Write down passages from familiar Big Books and poems from Shared Reading lessons on separate sheets of paper, replacing certain words with fill-in lines. Put a strip of magnetic tape above each line. Mount these sheets on cardboard or thick paper. Write each word deleted from the passage on a separate small card. Put a magnetic-tape strip on the back of each small card. Make an answer key for each selection. Keep everything for each passage or poem together in one plastic bag.

▲ Skills practiced:

Integrating meaning, structure, and visual cues

▲ What the children do:

1. Read the passage and try to figure out the missing word (or words).

2. Read the word cards and place the appropriate word on the blank line.

3. Check their work with the answer key.

Book Making ·······························

▲ Materials/preparation:

Pocket chart, small version of a familiar Big Book
Make copies of the pictures in the book. Rewrite the text on separate sentence strips. Mix up the

---

Teacher Tips

✳ Try to use only part of text from a Big Book, since including the entire book can be overwhelming for kindergartners. However, do use entire poems because the familiarity of the rhythm or pattern helps children figure out the missing words.

✳ Early in the year, you might want to draw pictures next to certain words to help children read the text and figure out the missing word.

✳ Increase the difficulty of this station as the year progresses by taking away letter or letter clusters for children to fill in instead of just words.

✳ Every time you finish reading a Big Book or poem, add it to this station and take away any texts that you feel children have mastered.

✳ Guess-and-check activities for homework will help reinforce the skills focused on at this station.

---

from the Big Book
Up in a Tree
by Joy Cowley

Up in a tree.

What do I see?

I see a bird

and it sees me.

pictures and sentence strips and put them in a plastic bag with the book.

▲ **Skills practiced:**
Integrating meaning, structure, and visual cues

▲ **What the children do:**
1. Read the text on the strips and match them to their appropriate pictures.
2. Put the story back together in correct sequential order in a pocket chart, on a table, or on the floor.
3. Check their work by rereading the book.

Matching text to pictures at the book-making station.

Overhead ·····················

To use at the end of the year

▲ **Materials/preparation:**
Overhead, overhead transparencies
Reproduce text from Shared Reading Big Books on transparencies.

▲ **Skills practiced:**
Fluency and phrasing

▲ **What the children do:**
1. Project a transparency.
2. Read the text.

Class News ·····················

To use throughout the year

Materials/preparation:
Envelopes, magnetic tape, magnetic boards
Cut up the daily class news—birthdays, trips, special occasions (written by one child every day on sentence strips) into phrases, words, endings, clusters of letters, or single letters at the beginning of words. Stick magnetic tape on the back of each cutting. Write the message on the outside of an envelope, and place the pieces inside.

Recreating the Class News

▲ **Skills practiced:**
One-to-one matching; directional movement; cross-checking cueing sources; self-monitoring and checking behaviors

59

▲ What the children do:

1. Arrange the news in its correct order on a magnetic board.

2. Check the front of the envelope to see if the arrangement is correct.

Listening Center ···

To use throughout the year

▲ Materials/preparation:

Audio tapes, tape recorder, tape player, small versions of Big Books
Tape-record your own versions of the Big Books you are using in Shared Reading.
Read the story three times, giving directions right on the tape (see scenario
below). This way you can target skills and words you are currently focusing on.
Label each tape with the book title and store it in its own plastic bag with the
corresponding small version of the Big Book.

▲ Skills practiced:

One-to-one matching; comprehension; locating supportive evidence in the text;
locating and framing quick-and-easy words; meaning and use of punctuation for
fluency and phrasing

▲ Teacher-Recorded Big Book Reading:

1. FIRST READING: *I'm going to read the story first. You can follow along as I read it
to you.*

2. SECOND READING: *This time, as I read the story, I want you to read along with
me and point to the words.* After reading the story through the second time,
then ask children to answer comprehension questions based on the story by
locating the evidence in the text. *Why did . . .? What happened when . . .? Talk
to your partner about your answer and see if you can find it in the story.* Give
them time to answer each question and then go over the answer with them,
going back to the page in the text that supports the answer. *The answer is . . .
Let's turn to page xx and read it together.* You might ask the children to turn
to a specific page and frame or locate a high-frequency word you've been
working on or to locate a specific punctuation mark.

3. THIRD READING: *Let's read the story again together, and we'll practice smooth
reading like we're talking.* Read the story. *Now turn off the tape player and read
the story on your own.*

Song and Poetry ···

To use throughout the year

▲ Materials/preparation:

The children use the poetry and song charts that are posted in the classroom.

▲ **Skills practiced:**

One-to-one matching; fluency and phrasing

▲ **What the children do:**

1. Go around to the past poetry and song charts that have been shared and posted in the classroom, pointing to the words as they read them.

| **Morning Messages** | ···

To use throughout the year

▲ **Materials/preparation:**

Business-size envelopes

Write the entire Morning Message (a brief text written with the children each morning) on the outside of an envelope. (See page 113 for a detailed description of Morning Messages.) Make another copy and cut apart the words. Some words will be highlighted from the Morning Message Lesson. Cut these words apart further, breaking the word up according to the highlighted chunk or part. For example, if the word were *thing* and you highlighted *ing*, you would cut it apart into *th* and *ing*, and if the word were *pool* you would divide it into *p* and *ool*. Put the parts inside the envelope.

▲ **Skills practiced:**

Integrating meaning, structure, and visual cues; identifying specific features within words

▲ **What the children do:**

1. Use the word parts to reconstruct the Morning Message.

2. Check their message with the outside of the envelope.

ALL ABOARD...
NEXT STOP READING PLAY STATIONS

To add to the fun of reading stations, I take pictures throughout the year of children working in the various stations. I give children their pictures with speech bubbles attached and ask them to describe what they were working on; I write their words in the bubble. Typical responses are, "I am making words with letters" or "I am reading Big Books." I post these pictures and descriptions outside our classroom to let parents and the school community know what we are working on.

The stations I've described are just the beginning. Make up your own stations by integrating what your students need with your own creativity and you'll enliven your classroom with fun activities for skill-building and independent learning.

Chapter Four

Zeroing in on Each Child with Guided Reading

Guided Reading is an important time of each kindergarten day. Small groups of five or six children with similar needs and abilities work with the teacher on text that addresses their particular needs. I usually begin my Guided Reading instruction in November, after the children have been introduced to necessary skills in Shared Reading lessons (Chapter Two) and have practiced them in Reading Play Stations (Chapter Three).

Each child in the group has his or her own copy of the book. Every group has its own basket of books that the children have read during past Guided Reading lessons. As I work with one group at a time, the rest of the class works in the Stations. (Before the children go to their stations, they practice smooth reading by rereading at least five of the books from their Guided Reading baskets.) The make-up of the groups is flexible, always changing according to the needs of each child.

During Guided Reading lessons, I reinforce the strategies I've taught in Shared Reading lessons. As the year progresses the groups read books at increasing levels of difficulty. As Shared and Guided Reading lessons mesh to help children gain literacy skills, children become independent problem-solvers.

GETTING READY FOR GUIDED READING

In their book *Apprenticeship in Literacy*, Dorn, French, and Jones list the beginning skills children need to be ready for Guided Reading. Using the following checklist is an excellent way to determine how ready your kindergarteners are. Do your students:

___ distinguish between text and illustration?

___ have some understanding of directionality?

___ have some knowledge of one-to-one matching?

___ know the difference between letters and words?

___ know the letters of the alphabet and a few high-frequency words, such as *I, the, a*?

___ actively participate in Shared Reading by predicting events and language structures that show an awareness of comprehension, rhythm, and rhyme?

___ spend time reading and noticing a few details of print?

___ explore the print on the classroom walls?

___ notice that the same words appear in many different contexts?

___ link sounds with symbols when they write?

___ articulate words slowly as they write?

When most of the students have gained these skills, you're ready to start setting up Guided Reading groups according to the children's abilities.

FORMING THE GROUPS

Shared and Independent Reading and Writing experiences in September and October help teach basic and emergent reading concepts that we'll focus on in Guided Reading groups. I also conduct a reading and writing assessment to gather information about the abilities of each child in my kindergarten class. The results help me to determine the make-up of my Guided Reading groups. I make three separate sheets that list specific reading and writing behaviors according to general ability level (Emergent 1, Emergent 2, and Emergent 3) and then assign each child to one of the three levels. Here's what's on each of the sheets (see pages 85–87 for reproducibles you can use for your class). You can use these sheets for reassessment all year long.

✹ Kindergarten Literacy Assessments

Guided Reading Assessment Checklist: Emergent 1
These children . . .

____ can identify some of the letters of the alphabet.

____ are inconsistent in letter-sound correspondence knowledge.

____ do not have control of one-to-one matching and directionality.

____ invent text according to picture cues.

____ write random strings of letters or marks for words.

____ can identify the front and back of a book.

Guided Reading Assessment Checklist: Emergent 2
These children . . .

____ can identify most of the letters of the alphabet (still have some confusion).

____ have some letter-sound knowledge.

____ are inconsistent with one-to-one matching and directionality (one line of text).

____ can write and read two-to-three high-frequency words (*I, a, go, the*).

____ participate in Shared Reading comprehension discussions, engage in choral reading of text, and can retell parts of the story.

____ can use picture cues when problem-solving unknown words.

____ record initial consonant sounds when writing words.

____ are aware of the front and back of a book and its title and author.

____ turn pages correctly and know that the left page precedes right page.

Guided Reading Assessment Checklist: Emergent 3
These children . . .

____ can identify letters of the alphabet (upper- and lower-case).

____ have letter-sound correspondence knowledge.

____ can write and read some high-frequency words (*I, a, the, go, see, to, my*).

____ are aware of the front and back of a book and its title and author.

____ turn pages correctly, knowing that the left page precedes right page.

____ can use picture cues to problem-solve unknown words and are beginning to look at a word's initial consonant within a line of text.

____ are beginning to grasp one-to-one matching and directionality (two lines of text).

____ are aware of the difference between a letter and a word.

____ can distinguish between text and illustrations.

____ are active participants in reading the text during Shared Reading—make predictions, comprehend text, retell stories, and engage in class discussions.

____ are beginning to articulate words slowly and record initial and final consonant sounds when writing.

After I group children by reading stages, I further organize the names into even more targeted groups. For example, if there are ten names on the Emergent 3 level sheet, I form two groups with five children in each. I match the children in each group as specifically as possible according to their similar strengths and needs.

Throughout the school year I continually assess my students and move them to appropriate groups depending on their individual needs. For example, if I notice that a child in one group is now able to read all the group's books accurately and fluently and comprehends the text more quickly than the other students, I'll move him into a group that's reading higher-level texts. However, I'll keep monitoring him to be sure that the new group is a good match for his abilities. Besides continually monitoring the progress and placement of every child in each group, I also re-evaluate and reflect on the groups as a whole every few weeks to make sure that my groups are meeting the needs of the class. If, for example, the whole group is reading fluently and accurately and comprehending books on a certain level, I will provide the group with a higher-level book that builds on the skills they've mastered.

ORGANIZING AND PLANNING
FOR GUIDED READING LESSONS

I have a two-pocket folder for each of my Guided Reading groups. In the pocket on one side, I keep an ongoing record sheet of all the books the group has read. The record sheet lists the date, title and level of the book. (See page 73 for a discussion of how the books are leveled.)

In the other pocket, I keep a planning sheet for each book the Guided Reading group is going to read during that session. In addition to the date, name of the group, and title and level of the book, my Guided Reading planning sheet includes planning

Guided-Reading Booklist

Group: The Pink House

Date	Title	Level
11/1	A Toy Box	A
11/2	Salad Vegetables	A
11/3	Christmas	A
11/6	The Birthday Party	A
11/7	Socks	A
11/8	Snowman	A
11/9	Treasure Hunt	A
11/10	Down to Town	A
11/13	We Go Out	A
11/14	The Ghost	A
11/15	Dressing Up	A
11/16	I Am	A

Guided Reading Planner

Date: 11/7　　　　Group: Pink House

Title of book: Socks

Level: A

Focus: One-to-one Matching (3 words on a page)

PLANNING Directionality
Significant words: dirty

Discussion Questions: What was the man doing in the story? What color socks did he hang on the line? Why was the man upset at the end of the story? Children will support their answers with evidence from the text.

Word study: THE, the, The - will make word with magnetic letters, write on wipe-off board and locate word within context. Word will be made in both upper and lower case.

Student's name	Observations	Teaching points
Jonathan	the red and blue socks the blue socks (p83)	Prompted to reread and check to see if what I read matches to text.
Amber	the yellow socks (p85)	(P) to look at picture
Emma	the pink socks the red socks	(P) to cross-check meaning with initial visual cues
Lili	Read accurately and fluently has one-to-one matching	
Carolina	the muddy socks the dirty socks (p9)	(P) what would you expect to see in the beginning of the word
	*validated to child that her response made sense	muddy (P) to check word Does that look right?

* second rereading for fluency + phrasing

My planning and record-keeping sheets for Guided Reading; see templates on pages 88–89.

notes: a specific focus that I'll be working on during the session, significant words to introduce, discussion questions, and a word-study emphasis. I make sure to have space to note individual students' names, my observations, and the teaching points I made.

Strategy Focus: I base my focus on what I've observed during previous Guided Reading, Shared Reading, and Reading Play Station sessions. As my kindergartners gain skills during the year, I update the focus to keep it in line with their current needs. The chart on page 67 provides a general idea of how the strategy focus may develop through the year. I'm always reinforcing strategies taught earlier while adding more advanced ones. If you cover all these skills and strategies, you'll have provided a firm literacy foundation for your kindergartners.

Significant Words: Before each Guided Reading lesson, I choose one or two "significant" words from the book we're going to read. These are words that may not be familiar to the children or are not part of the group's background knowledge. Or they may be words I think the students may have difficulty figuring out on their own by using meaning, visual, and structural cueing. For example, I might introduce the word *hedgehog* from the book *Hedgehog Is Hungry* by Beverly Randell (Rigby) as a significant word for inner-city school children because it is likely that they wouldn't know about hedgehogs. I may also point out significant phrases for the same reasons. I point out the words and phrases as I introduce the book (see page 69).

Discussion Questions: In advance of a Guided Reading lesson, I list comprehension questions that I may ask after children read their book. These questions involve:

◆ **sequencing of events:** *What happened at the beginning . . . middle . . . end of the story?*

◆ **identifying the facts:** *Who is . . .? What were . . .? Where did . . .? When was . . .?*

◆ **locating evidence:** *Where in the story . . .? How did you know . . .? How come . . .?*

◆ **confirming or correcting predictions:** *Were we right about . . .? Why . . .?*

◆ **asking inferential questions:** *Why do you think . . .?*

◆ **setting a purpose for reading:** *Let's read and see if . . .?*

◆ **relating personal experiences to the text:** *Does that remind you of something in your life?*

◆ **discussing the components of a story:** *What do you notice about (character, setting, plot, problem/solution) . . .?*

Guided Reading Strategy Focus Throughout the Year

Nov/Dec	Jan/Feb	Mar/Apr	May/June
Use picture to predict text	Understand return sweep	Self-monitor to see if what was read makes sense, sounds right, and looks right (notices errors)	Integrate meaning, structural, and visual cues
Locate where to begin reading	Reread to clarify confusions	Self-correct	Self-correct
Understand directionality	Notice if what is read doesn't match text	Reread	Problem solve through analogy (use the known to get to the unknown) and search for known features within words—clusters *str, fr*
Turn pages correctly	Cross-check meaning with visual cues (initial letters of words)	Cross-check meaning and structural cues with visual cues (going across word looking for chunks and parts of words—*th, sh, ch, wh*)	Apply and integrate reading strategies to higher-level texts
Differentiate between a letter and word	Develop a bank of high-frequency words	Develop fluency and phrasing	Verbalize how to use reading strategies
Match letters and words one-to-one	Read and locate known words within a variety of texts	Understand the meaning and use of quotation marks and ellipses	
Locate and frame known high-frequency words and letters within a word	Begin to understand the meaning and use of periods, question marks, and exclamation points	Increase sight vocabulary	
Use known initial letters to figure out unknown words	Able to recognize sentence beginnings and endings		
Identify capital letters, periods, and spaces between words			
Begin to develop fluency and phrasing			
Make predictions based on title and pictures			
Understand the meaning of author and illustrator			
Recognize story patterns			

Word Study: To plan a word-study component for a Guided Reading lesson, I choose a word from the story that has features we've been working on—quick-and-easy words, word endings, chunking, and so on (see page 72).

Observation and Assessment: During the Guided Reading lesson, I use my planning sheet to make relevant notes. As I work with each student, I note the student's name, comment on his or her reading behaviors, and jot down the teaching prompts I used with the students to help them read the words they didn't know. Reviewing these comments later helps direct my plans for instruction and enables me to choose appropriate focal points for future lessons. The kinds of notes I make during a Guided Reading session tell me whether or not the child always asks for help. My notes will also indicate which of the following strategies she has internalized:

◆ uses picture cues.

◆ has mastered one-to-one matching.

◆ knows where to begin reading.

◆ has mastered directionality and return sweep.

◆ rereads to figure out an unknown word or rereads to see if what he/she just read makes sense, sounds right, and looks right.

◆ is beginning to self-monitor, notices errors.

◆ makes self-corrections.

◆ makes substitutions that are visually similar, structurally or grammatically correct, and meaningful.

◆ cross-checks one cue against another.

◆ integrates cueing sources (meaning, structure, visual).

◆ reads with fluency and phrasing.

◆ understands the meaning and use of punctuation marks.

◆ stretches out words (looking at the beginning, middle, and ending parts of a word).

◆ looks for known parts in words.

◆ breaks down words into parts.

◆ uses analogy to problem-solve an unknown word.

◆ uses the pattern in the story to help figure out an unknown word.

◆ has a full understanding of the text.

◆ reads and locates high-frequency words.

WHAT HAPPENS DURING A GUIDED READING LESSON

Before I begin each Guided Reading lesson, and while the group is rereading familiar books from their Guided Reading basket, I select one child and take a running record, a written transcript of that child's reading behaviors (discussed later in this chapter and more fully in Chapter Six), using the book I introduced to the group the day before. Then I proceed through the following lesson sequence.

❋ Book Introduction

Each child takes a copy of the book I've selected for the lesson. Before they begin reading, we look at the book—the title and the pictures—to get a general sense of what it's about. I begin by focusing the group's attention on the one or two significant words or phrases I've chosen to concentrate on for this book and any repetitive language patterns in the story. With this advance preparation, students can combine the new words with some already familiar words and word parts as they read. As we look through the pictures, I stop on the pages with the significant words and introduce them to the group in a way that fits into the context of the story. I say the word and ask what letters the students would expect to see at the beginning of that word. They respond, and each child uses that information to locate the word within the text of his or her book. After they locate the word, they run their finger underneath the word as they read it.

Next we look briefly at the pictures on each page, and I guide students in a discussion of what they think is happening in the story. I make sure that they're actively engaged in the conversation. As the year progresses and children read higher-level texts, my introduction becomes a little less detailed. I may introduce part of the book and have children predict what's going to happen at the end of the story. Or I may give the group a specific question to think about as they're reading. These before-reading prompts encourage children to set a purpose for reading—to find meaning in the text—before they actually read the story.

❋ Reading With Teacher Prompting

Now that children have some familiarity with the book, they open their copies and begin to read out loud at their own pace. They may start by reading the title, author, illustrator, and title page as we do during Shared Reading. While children are reading on their own, I go to each child and listen as he or she reads. As I observe children's reading behaviors, I provide prompts to help them problem solve words they get stuck on by suggesting strategies from Shared Reading. I try to tailor my suggestions to each student by choosing the strategy I think would best suit his

Guided Reading Prompts

STRATEGIES	PROMPTS
One-to-One Matching	• Read it with your finger. • Check to see if what you read matches the words in the book. • Were there enough words?
Self-Monitoring	• Were you right? • Why did you stop? • I liked how you stopped reading. You knew that it didn't make sense, sound right, or look right.
Self-Correcting	• Try that again. • Were you right? • How did you know that the word was _____ ? • What letter would you expect to see at the beginning of the word _____ and at the end of the word _____ ? • Check it. Does it look right? • Reread the sentence and see if you can figure out the tricky part. • I like how you corrected yourself. You knew that didn't make sense. You reread the sentence, and I saw you looking at the picture and at the beginning part of the word.
Using Meaning Cues	• Think about the story. Does that make sense? • Look at the pictures to help you figure out the word. • What's happening in the story so far? • Reread and think about what word would make sense here?
Using Structure Cues	• Does that sound right? • What is another word that could fit here? Check to see if that word looks right and sounds right. • Does that sound like the way we talk?
Using Visual Cues	• Does that look right? • Write the word _____ (the substituted word that the child said). Does that look like the word _____? (Point to the word on the line of text.) • Do you know another word that begins with the same letters or ends with the same letters? • What would you expect to see at the beginning or ending of the word? • Do you notice any chunks in that word? • What chunk do you hear at the end of that word? • Do you know any parts of that word? • Run your fingers across the word and say it slowly. • Do you know another word that has the same chunk as this word? You know the word (*day*). Can you write it? How are these two words the same? If you know (*day*) then you can get to (*play*). Is that word (*play*)? (Point to the word within line of text.) • Can you frame the word _____ ?
Cross-Checking and Integrating Cues	• It could be _____ that makes sense. What would you expect to see at the beginning or ending of that word? Does that look right? • Before you begin to read, check yourself to make sure that whatever you read makes sense and looks right. • The word you just said looks like _____ , but think about the story. Would that word make sense? • How did you know that the word was _____ ? • Check to see if what you just read makes sense, looks right, and sounds right.
Fluency and Phrasing	• Read smoothly like you're talking. • Check the end of the sentence for the punctuation marks. If there's a question mark, we'll read it in a questioning voice. If there is an exclamation mark, we'll read the sentence in an excited voice. And if there's a period, we'll stop for a moment.

adapted from *Reading Recovery: A Guidebook for Teachers in Training* by Marie Clay (Heinemann, 1993) and *Guided Reading* by Irene Fountas and Gay Su Pinnell, (Heinemann, 1996)

or her particular strengths and weaknesses. My goal is to help students develop their own menu of strategies to use to create meaning from print. While I make the rounds, I briefly note my observations and suggested strategies on my Guided Reading planning sheet.

As a trained Reading Recovery teacher, I use the prompts that Marie Clay promotes and supports in *Reading Recovery: A Guidebook for Teachers in Training* (1993). You can also find effective prompts in *Guided Reading* by Irene Fountas and Gay Su Pinnell (1996). I always start out with a higher level prompt such as, "What can you try?" However, if the child can't figure out the word, I suggest the specific prompt that targets the strategy or behavior I'm trying to encourage.

Your goal toward the end of the school year is to prompt less as children internalize the strategies and begin to problem-solve on their own more and make corrections.

❀ Group Reflection

After each child reads the book individually, gather the group together to take stock. Focus on problem solving, comprehension, and fluency and phrasing.

Problem Solving: Choose one or two powerful teaching points that you mentioned during the individual conferences. Share with the group the problem-solving strategies you noticed individual students using. For example:

Teacher: *When I was reading with John, at first he said the word* duck *instead of* bird. *He went back reread the sentence and corrected himself. How did you know that the word wasn't* duck, *John?*

John: Duck *starts with a* d *and the word starts with a* b. *Also there is a picture of a bird.*

Teacher: *That's just what good readers do. They check to see if what they said makes sense and looks right. Great job!*

You may ask the other students to share problem-solving strategies they used. The child describes the strategy she used and tells us where in the story she used it. We find the appropriate page of the story and turn to it. Showing the relevant text, the child explains again how she figured out the word.

Comprehension: Next you can ask the children some comprehension questions, such as "*Why did the children feel ill at the end of the story?*" Have them support their answers with evidence from the text. They turn to the specific page, find the information, and read it to the group.

Fluency and Phrasing: At the beginning of the school year, I have children in

Guided Reading groups read the book a second time to develop fluency and proper phrasing. Tell children that they're reading the book again in order to practice smooth reading. Read together in unison. You should have second readings throughout the year, whenever you notice that a reading group needs practice with fluency.

Word Study: At the end of the lesson, concentrate on word-study skills. During beginning-of-the-year lessons, have children practice specific quick-and-easy words in the story. You might give each child a wipe-off board, a magnetic board, and a set of the magnetic letters that are in the word, *the*, for example. Model making *the* with magnetic letters and then ask the children to locate *the* in their copy of the text and make it with their magnetic letters. The children can then write *the* on their wipe-off boards. It's beneficial to have the children make the word with all capital letters, with all lower-case letters, and with an initial capital letter and the rest lower case. They should understand that their knowledge of the word is stable, that *the* is still *the* no matter how it's written.

Make the Most of Your Letters
If you don't have enough letters or boards, use one magnetic board and have each child take a turn making the word. As one child makes the word, the others write it and then find it within the text.

It's also a good idea to discuss the features of the word. How many letters are in the word? What is the first letter? The last?

In my class, once children know a quick-and-easy word, I begin to teach them in subsequent lessons how to problem solve words using chunking. For example, if they know the word *went* and it's in the story, I show them how to get to *sent* and *tent*. They form these words with the magnetic letters on their own boards and then write them on their own wipe-off boards. While this is generally used as a whole-class experience, applying the skills I've modeled during Shared Reading to this Guided Reading instruction helps children problem solve words later when they're reading and writing on their own.

I usually preplan a word-study activity, but sometimes I scrap the plan and shift to something I notice children are having difficulty with during the lesson. For example, once I planned an *ay* chunking lesson because I thought children would have trouble with the word *away*. While they were reading, I noticed that they were stuck on the quick-and-easy word *was*. So I shifted gears and concentrated on *was*. Altering a prepared lesson to respond to students' immediate needs is an important aspect of good teaching.

Follow-Up Activities: Every day before children go to their specific reading stations or literacy activities, they read five books from their basket. This gives them the opportunity to practice problem-solving strategies as well as fluent reading.

For additional practice, each day you can have the children take home and read two books: the book that the group read that day and a book that's familiar from past readings. Prepare and send home an activity sheet for the new book. It might include a simple question about the story and an activity to provide practice with the word-study skill you focused on in the lesson; see sample at right.

Sometimes I provide a word-study activity using chunking or take three sentences from the book and delete words that we focused on and have children fill in the words. At the beginning of the year, I tell the parents to encourage children to stretch out the words and write the sounds they hear.

As the year progresses, I ask children to do some writing at home, and I tell the parents to write whatever children can't write for themselves. I might ask children to write about how this story reminded them of something that happened in their own lives, or to write about their favorite part. Toward the end of the year, I ask them write a retelling of the story, or to describe their favorite character. Later in the year, children become increasingly able to write on their own, and I make sure the level and type of home activity reflect their progress.

Name_____

Title: <u>The Hungry Kitten</u>

Write three words that sound the same and have the same chunk as the word *day*

1._____

2._____

3._____

What was your favorite part of the story?

_____

_____

Draw a picture of your favorite part.

CHOOSING BOOKS FOR GUIDED READING

It's important to choose books—not too easy, not too difficult—that match the current skills and abilities in your Guided Reading groups but challenge them. If the texts are too difficult, children become easily frustrated and lose their confidence as readers, and then it's almost impossible for the teacher to introduce strategies that will help them become better readers. If a text is too easy, children will not be challenged to build on what they've already learned. I choose books that contain familiar text as well as one or two new teaching points that I bring to the group's attention. Here are tools to make the process easy.

Leveling: To choose the appropriate books, you'll need to place them in predetermined, coded levels ("level" them) according to a range of skills within a grade level that have been developed by reading experts or jointly by schools. Some schools have a book room with sets of texts that have already been leveled by other teachers who've used them in their classrooms. Also, published lists of a wide variety of books from many publishers are available to help with the leveling task. You can level books on

your own by using one of the published guides to choose appropriate books and then ordering the books in sets that come with six copies per set. I use Irene C. Fountas & Gay Su Pinnell's guide entitled *Matching Books to Readers* (1999). It lists and indicates levels for 7,500 books to use with kindergarten to third-grade children.

I stay on a level as long as it meets the children's needs, dropping down a level if the book is too hard or moving up a level if it's too easy. However, I've found that if the level is right, it's important to take your time and not rush through it. I have the groups read a minimum of 15–20 books on a particular level. Every book on each level provides many great teaching opportunities. On the other hand, I make sure I keep the books in the baskets fresh. So, as the weeks go by, I take out the books that are too easy or that the children have lost interest in. To select the specific books within a level and plan your skill focus, refer to the guide provided below.

What Should I Look for in Guided Reading Books?

Once you know the specific level that children are reading at in their Guided Reading books, you can look through several books on that level and choose one that matches the needs of your students. For instance, if you want children to practice the strategy of cross-checking meaning with visual cues, choose a book that contains words with strong initial sounds that clearly correspond to specific illustrations. The following questions are helpful in examining a text and determining if it is appropriate for the reader:

- How many pages and words does the book have?
- How many lines are on a page? How long are the sentences?
- Is the storyline simple or complex (with many characters and events)?
- Do the illustrations strongly support the text or must the children get meaning by paying close attention to the print?
- Are there repeating sentence patterns?
- Does the print appear at the same place on every page or is the layout varied?
- Is the structure of the language natural and uncomplicated?
- How many words are known high-frequency words and how many are new and challenging words?
- Are there familiar words the children have encountered in previous texts?
- What punctuation is used? Is there dialogue?
- Is the print big enough? Is there enough space between words so the children can point and read?
- Can the children personally relate to the topic?
- Are the words longer with inflectional endings (*ing, ed, s*)?
- Are there changes in tense (past, present)?
- Does the reading vocabulary encourage word analysis, such as taking words apart and using what the child knows about one word to get to another word?

Adapted from *Matching Books to Readers*, Fountas and Pinnell (Heinemann, 1999)

Running Records: Along with targeting appropriate levels and analyzing the book's specific characteristics, I base my decisions about book choices on my observations of children as they read. These include observations I note on the Guided Reading planning sheet, and the detailed running records—the written transcript of exactly what the child says when he or she is reading a Guided Reading book (see page 102). I take running records during Independent Reading and before I begin Guided Reading. As the Guided Reading group is rereading books from their baskets, I select one child and take a running record of his or her reading of the book I introduced to the group the day before. I study the running records as one more way to evaluate whether or not I'm on target with the book's level. In addition, running records may guide me to move a child whose skills are out of sync with the others in his group to another group.

A SAMPLE GUIDED READING LESSON—*THE GHOST*

Following is an example of a beginning-of-the-year, Guided Reading lesson for the book *The Ghost* by Joy Cowley.

✺ Planning

Choosing the book: The level of *The Ghost*, according to Fountas and Pinnell, is *A*, a beginning kindergarten level. I chose this particular level *A* book because the illustrations support the text and the layout is consistent throughout the book. The print is at the bottom of the page with the pictures above it. The one line of text on each page supports one-to-one matching. The repetitive pattern, *I see the _____* throughout the book enables children to read with confidence. The quick-and-easy word *the* helps children with one-to-one matching as they follow along with the text.

Guided Reading Planner

Date: 11/15   Group: Pink House

Title of book: The Ghost

Level: A

Focus: Cross-Checking Meaning with Initial Visual Cues/one-to-i Matching (4-5 words within one line of text)

PLANNING

Significant words: Chairs   Mom   Dad

Discussion Questions: What are some of the things that the girl saw through her mask? What happened to Mom and Dad at the end of the story? Why is the story called The Ghost? (Support answers with evidence from the text)

Word study: Making, locating and writing the word [see] [see]

Student's name	Observations	Teaching points
Jonathan	stars (pg. 3) window	(P) to Cross-check meaning and visual cues Used Steven's name to get to st
Amber	I see the black cat I see the cat (pg. 5)	(P) to point to words and check to see if what read matches to text.
Emma	I see mother I see Mom (pg. 7) beginning to self-monitor	(R) Why did you stop? (knew the word wasn't right). (P) to check ending of word-like Jennifer's name? (er)
Lili	Read very well- has control over 1-1 matching. Comprehended story· located evidence within text.	
Carolina	I see a door I see the door	(R) to reread sentence and write the word (a) on wipe-off board
* Second rereading for fluency and phrasing		(P) to check and see if there is the word (a) in that sentence.

Choosing significant words and word-study skills: I chose to work on the high-frequency word *see*, which was a new word for the students. I wanted them to gain fluency in reading, writing, and locating *see*. I also chose to introduce the words *chairs*, and *Mom* and *Dad* to the group in advance. Even though the pictures in the book generally support the text, those that correspond to those words do not. The chair in the illustration could be a couch, and the parents could be identified as a man and lady. I didn't want the children to be confused.

I also wanted the children to become familiar with the *ch* digraph. During our class morning meeting, we had noticed the *ch* sound from Charlie's name and read the digraph on a chart that we recite from every day. This chart includes pictures of a checkmark, a thumb, a shoe, and a wheel. Next to each picture are the corresponding letters that make the beginning sound of each object (*sh, ch, th, wh*).

Choosing the focus: For this lesson, I focused on one-to-one matching and cross-checking meaning and initial letter visual cues because I'd noticed that the children in this group relied mainly on picture cues to figure out words they didn't know. I wanted them to begin using the print or visual cues in a word. Before the children read the book, I explained that I wanted them to problem solve words by first looking at the initial letter and then checking their prediction of what the word might be with the illustration. I used a page from *The Farm*, a Big Book they were already familiar with from a past Shared Reading lesson to demonstrate the strategy they'd be working on.

As I always do, I went over what I planned to say in my mind. For example, I planned to say, *I've noticed that when you're reading you use the pictures to help you figure out the words. That's a good thing to do, but it's also important to look at the word. Remember when we read the Big Book* The Farm (*showing page from* The Farm), *and I covered up the word* birds? *We checked the picture first, and a lot of you said the covered-up word was* ducks *because the picture looks like there were a bunch of ducks. But then, remember how I pointed out the first letter of the word and we saw that it was a* b *and we knew that the word couldn't be* ducks *because it started with a* b *not a* d. *So today, when you're reading, make sure you check the picture and the first letter of the word.*

With the lesson prepared and my planning sheet ready to record observations, I called the group together to join me in a circle of chairs (sometimes it's around a table or on the carpet), and I handed out a copy of the new book to each child. Here's how the introduction to the book and the conferences with individual children proceeded:

✸ Lesson Scenario

Ms. Franzese: Today we're going to read a book called The Ghost. Let's point to the title as we read it. What do you see on the front cover of the book?

Jonathan: I see a girl with a white sheet around her.

Amber: She's looking in the mirror.

Ms. Franzese: What did she make out of the paper bag?

Emma: She made a ghost mask. She's dressing up like a ghost.

Ms. Franzese: Let's turn to the title page. Let's read the title together as we point to the words. What is that a picture of?

Lili: It's the girl in her ghost costume. She's putting the mask on top of her head.

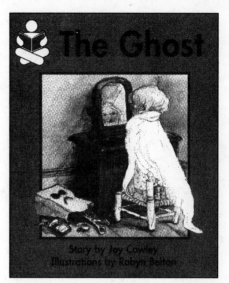

The Ghost by Joy Cowley, illustrated by Robyn Belton. Copyright (c) 1998 by The Wright Group. Reprinted by permission of The Wright Group, 19201 120th Avenue NE, Bothell, WA 98011-9512.1-800-523-2371.

(The children turn to page 2)

Ms. Franzese: Look at the shape of the picture on this page. Let's turn back to the title page and look at the eyes of the girl's mask. How are both pictures the same?

Carolina: The picture is in the shape of the eyes of the mask.

Ms. Franzese: Why do you think the pictures are shaped that way?

Carolina: Because the girl has the mask on and she's looking through it.

Ms. Franzese: That's right. This book is going to tell us all the things that she sees with her mask on. Let's look through the book to find out all the things she sees through her mask.

(The children turn back to page 2)

Ms. Franzese: What does she see?

Amber: The door.

Ms. Franzese: Right. She says, "I see the door." Now let's look at the other things she sees. What does she see next?

Lili: The window and the cat.

Emma: *Now she sees the table and the cat and the whole room.*

Ms. Franzese: *That is a room, but she sees the chairs in the room. What would you expect to see at the beginning of the word chairs, like check (I refer to chart in room)?*

All: Ch

Ms. Franzese: *Can you find the word chairs? Run your fingers across the word and say it.*

(The children locate word chairs in the text)

Ms. Franzese: *Now what does the girl see?*

Lili: *She sees a man and a lady.*

Ms. Franzese: *The man and the lady are her Mom and Dad. What letter would you expect to see in the beginning of the word Mom?*

Lili: *An M.*

Ms. Franzese: *How about at the end of the word Mom?*

Lili: M.

Ms. Franzese: *Find the word Mom and run your fingers across it and say it. (I write the word on the wipe-off board or form the word with magnetic letters.)*

Ms. Franzese: *What would you expect to see in the beginning and ending of the word Dad?*

Amber: D.

(The children locate the word Dad in the text.)

Ms. Franzese: *Where do you think the girl is?*

Jonathan: *She is in her house.*

Ms. Franzese: *How did you know that?*

Jonathan: *Because she sees all of the things that are in a house, like chairs, a table, and a cat.*

Ms. Franzese: *What do you think she's going to do when she sees her Mom and Dad?*

Amber: *Take off her mask?*

Lili	*Ask if see could go trick or treating.*
Carolina:	*She's going to scare them.*
Ms. Franzese:	*Let's turn the page and find out.*

(The children turn the page.)

Carolina:	*She scares them.*
Ms. Franzese:	*What do you think she said?*
Carolina:	*Boo!*
Ms. Franzese:	*That's right. She said "Boo!" I've noticed that when you're reading, you use the pictures to help you figure out the words. That's a good thing to do, but it's also important to look at the word like we did with* chair, mom *and* dad. *Remember when we read the Big Book* The Farm *and I covered up the word* birds? *(I take out* The Farm *and show children the page.)*
	We checked the picture first and a lot of you said the covered-up word is ducks *because the picture seemed to show a bunch of ducks. But then I showed you the first letter of the word and we saw that it was a* b *and we knew that the word couldn't be* ducks *because it started with a* b *not a* d. *So today when you're reading, make sure you check the picture and the first letter of the word to see if the word looks right and makes sense to you. After you finish reading the book on your own, you can read the book together with someone in the group. I'll come around and listen to you read. If you aren't reading with me, and you've finished reading* The Ghost, *choose some of your favorite books from your basket to read on your own.*

Here are conversations I had with individual children as I circulated among them and observed their reading of *The Ghost*.

Jonathan reads:

Jonathan:	I see the stars. (The text reads: *I see the window.*)
Ms. Franzese:	*That does make sense because there are stars in the picture. But what letters would you expect to see at the beginning of the word* stars? *Like in Steven's name?*
Jonathan:	st.

Ms. Franzese: *Does that look right?*
(I direct Jonathan's attention to the printed word *window*.)

Jonathan: *No, this word starts with a w.*

Ms. Franzese: *What word could fit there that would make sense and start with a w?*

Jonathan: (Jonathan rereads the sentence and cross-checks the meaning with a visual cue.) I see the window. *It's window. There's a picture of a window and the word starts with a w.*

Ms. Franzese: *Great! I liked how you reread the sentence and checked the word* window *to see if it made sense in the story and if it looked right.*

Amber reads:

Amber: I see the black cat.
(The text reads: *I see the cat.*)

Ms. Franzese: *Reread the sentence and point to each word as you read it. Check to see if what you say matches the words on the page*

Amber: (Amber rereads sentence, pointing to the words.)
I, see, the, and cat match one-to-one. But there's no black. It doesn't say black.

Ms. Franzese: *Good checking!*

Emma reads:

Emma: I see mother.
(The text reads: *I see Mom.*)
(After Emma reads *I see mother*, she pauses and self-monitors.)

Ms. Franzese: *Why did you stop?*

Emma: *I don't think that was right.*

Ms. Franzese: *That's great that you stopped because you didn't think the word was right. Let's check it. What letter would you expect to see at the beginning of the word Mother?*

Emma: *An M.*

Ms Franzese: *Is that right?* (I point to the word)

Emma: *Yes, that's an M.*

Ms. Franzese: *What letters would you expect to see at the end of the word* mother, *like in Jennifer's name?*

Emma: er.
(Emma checks the ending of the of the word.)
But there's an m at the end of this word.

Ms. Franzese: *What word would make sense in this sentence that starts with an M and ends with an M?*

Emma: (Emma rereads the sentence)
I see Mom. *The word is* Mom.

Carolina reads:

Carolina: I see a door.
(The text reads: *I see the door.*)

Ms. Franzese: *Can you write the word* a *on the wipe-off board? You read* I see a door. *Reread the sentence and check to see if there is the word* a *in that sentence.*

Carolina: (Carolina writes and checks for the quick-and-easy word.)
I see the door. *The word is* the *not* a.

Ms. Franzese: *Good readers check to see if what they read looks right. Good reading, Carolina.*

Lili reads:

Lili: (Lili reads the whole book accurately and fluently.)

Ms. Franzese: *Lili, I love the way you read so smoothly, like you're talking.*

After I read with each child in the group, I gather the children together, and we discuss some of the good problem-solving strategies various children used while they read. I begin the session by sharing all of the good reading behaviors I observed and asking children if they used the focus strategy, cross-checking meaning with initial visual cues, that we discussed before reading the book. The children in the group describe what they did to figure out an unknown word.

Ms. Franzese: *While I was reading with Jonathan, he checked the picture and the beginning of the word. Jonathan, could you tell us what you did when you were reading page 3?*

(The children turn to page 3.)

Jonathan: *First I read* I see the stars. *Then I looked at the word, and I saw that it started with a* w *not with an* st. *The word is* window *because it starts with a* w *and there is a picture of a window.*

Ms. Franzese:	Did anyone else do any problem solving when you tried to figure out an unknown word?
Emma:	I read Mother. Then I went back and there was no er at the end, like in Jennifer's name. It was an m, so it was Mom.
Ms. Franzese:	So you corrected yourself by checking the ending of the word. That's what good readers do! What were some of the things that the girl saw through her mask?
Lili:	A cat, chairs, and Mom and Dad.
Ms. Franzese:	Where could you find those in the book?

(Lili locates the evidence in the story by turning to the appropriate pages and reading the sentences that supports her answer.)

Ms. Franzese:	What happened to Mom and Dad at the end of the story?
Carolina:	They got scared because the girl said "Boo!" They thought she was a ghost.
Ms. Franzese:	Were our predictions right about what the girl would do at the end of the story?
Carolina:	Mine was right. She did scare her Mom and Dad.
Lili:	But she didn't go trick or treating or take off her mask.
Ms. Franzese:	Why was this story called The Ghost?
Emma:	Because the girl in the story dressed up like a ghost. She put a mask on and saw things in her house. Then she scared her Mom and Dad.

Next I worked with the children on the words and word study.

Ms. Franzese: Let's turn to page 2. Now, frame the word see.

(The children use their two index fingers to isolate the word see in the sentence, with one finger at the beginning of the word and the other at the end. I make the word see with magnetic letters on a board.)

Ms. Franzese:	How many letters are in this word?
Jonathan:	Three.
Ms. Franzese:	What are the letters in the word?
All:	s/e/e.
Ms. Franzese:	What is the first letter in the word, and what is the last letter?

All: s *and* e.

(I make the word with all capital letters *SEE* as well as a capital letter and lower-case letters *See*.)

Ms. Franzese: *What is this word?*

Lili: *The word is* see. *It just has capital letters.*

Ms. Franzese: *So the word is still* see *even if it's in capital or lower case letters?*

All: *Yes!*

(I mix up the letters and a child makes the word see. As one child makes the word, the others write it and locate it on the page in the story. The children take turns making the word with magnetic letters. If you have enough boards and letters each child can get a set of letters and boards and they can simultaneously write, form, and locate the word see.)

Ms. Franzese: *Now we're going to read the book* The Ghost *together to practice our smooth reading.*

❋ Follow-Up Activities

The children took home the Guided Reading book, *The Ghost*, and practiced reading it with an adult. I also gave the group a response sheet on which I wrote the new quick-and-easy word *see* from the story, and asked them to practice writing it once, using Diane Snowball's *Look, Say, Name, Cover, Write* technique (see Chapter Nine). I also ask the question: "What did the girl see?" on the homework sheet. Children fill in missing words from the story.

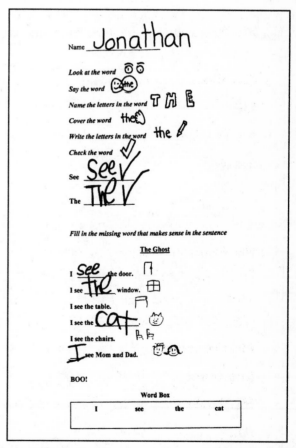

Homework sheet to accompany rereading of Guiding Reading book at home

SEE HOW THEY GROW—
THROUGHOUT THE YEAR

Shown below are two planned Guided Reading lessons that I taught at the beginning and end of the school year for one Guided Reading group. (While Guided Reading groups are flexible and can change, sometimes they stay the same throughout the year. These planning sheets are for a group that stayed intact.) Notice that as the levels of text increase in difficulty, the focus of each lesson, types of comprehension questions, and word-study work become a bit more complex.

As the text levels increase, I provide less information during the book introduction. For example, sometimes as children are discussing a story during the introduction, I'll stop before the last two pages and give them a purpose question to think about as they're reading the book.

Notice in my observational comments how children grow from being routinely prompted to problem-solve to integrating cueing sources on their own. In November, the group started on a level A, the beginning kindergarten level, and by the end of the school year, they were reading books on Level G, which is equivalent to the middle/end of first grade. They moved up seven levels. Most kindergarten Guided Reading groups gain at least four levels by the end of the year.

Guided Reading Planner

Date: 11/7   Group: Pink House

Title of book: Socks

Level: A

Focus: One-to-one Matching (3 words on a page)
Directionality

PLANNING
Significant words: dirty

Discussion Questions: What was the man doing in the story? What color socks did he hang on the line? Why was the man upset at the end of the story? (children will support their answers with evidence from the text)

Word study: THE, the, The - will make word with magnetic letters, write on wipe-off board and locate word within context. Word will be made in both upper and

Student's name	Observations	Teaching points
Jonathan (pg.3)	the red and blue socks / the blue socks (top)	Prompted to reread and check to see if what I read matches to text.
Amber (pg.5)	the _yellow_ socks	(P) to look at picture
Emma	the pink socks / the red socks	(P) to cross-check meaning with initial visual cues
Lili	Read accurately and fluently / has one-to-one matching	
Carolina (pg.8)	the muddy socks / the dirty socks	(P) what would you expect to see in the beginning of the word
	* validated to child that her response made sense	muddy (P) to check word Does that look right?

* second Rereading for fluency + phrasing

Guided Reading Planner

Date: 6/8   Group: Pink House

Title of book: Noise

Level: G

Focus: Integration of Cue Sources (Meaning·Structure·Vis. Meaning & Use of Punctuation Mark) Confirming and unconfirming words

PLANNING
Significant words: listen, stereo Phrase: Yakka, dukka Yakka dukka yak, yak

Discussion Questions: Setting A Purpose for Reading. During the book introduction stop at page 13 and tell the students to read to find out if the children are going to continue to stay quiet and listen to things →

Word study: Word Endings - Use a the known word (look) to teach endings look → looks → looking → looked. Children will locate listen - listening and listened in story

Student's name	Observations	Teaching points
Jonathan (pg.2)	Julie had the music on / Julie had the radio on	Made self-correction. Validated that child integrated 3 cueing sources.
Amber (pg.10)	They listen and listen / They listened and listened	(P) to check ending of words
Emma (pg.8)	Not a thing	(P) what parts of the word do you know? Noticed (ing) with like trust reread sentence to make sure word makes sense in sentence
Lili (pg.14)	They on / Then on	(P) Child reread and self-correct. He states "Didn't sound right - It's then not they
Carolina (pg.5)	Mom said / Mom yelled	(P) What would you expect to see in the beginning of said? (P) What word would make sense, look right and sound right?
	Carolina checks word after prompting. She figured out the word	(P) to look at exclamation mark in previous sentence "Stop that Noise!" Discuss meaning of exclamation point

* Children comprehended story very well. Located answers in text.

Guided Reading Assessment Checklist—Emergent 1

These children . . .

_____ can identify some of the letters of the alphabet.

_____ are inconsistent in letter-sound correspondence knowledge.

_____ do not have control of one-to-one matching and directionality.

_____ invent text according to picture cues.

_____ write random strings of letters or marks for words.

_____ can identify the front and back of the book.

Guided Reading Assessment Checklist—Emergent 2

These children . . .

_____ can identify most of the letters of the alphabet (still have some confusions).

_____ have some letter-sound knowledge

_____ are inconsistent with one-to-one matching and directionality (one line of text).

_____ can write and read two-to-three high-frequency words (*I, a, go, the*).

_____ participate in Shared Reading comprehension discussions, engage in choral reading of text, and can retell parts of the story.

_____ can use picture cues when problem-solving unknown words.

_____ when writing words, record initial consonant sounds.

_____ are aware of the front and back of the book, title, and author.

_____ turn pages correctly and know that the left page precedes right page.

Reading and Writing in Kindergarten   Scholastic Professional Books

Guided Reading Assessment Checklist—Emergent 3

These children . . .

_____ can identify letters of the alphabet (upper- and lower-case).

_____ have letter-sound correspondence knowledge.

_____ can write and read some high-frequency words (*l, a, the, go, see, to, my*).

_____ are aware of the front and back of the book, title, and author.

_____ can turn pages correctly, knowing that the left page precedes right page.

_____ can use picture cues to problem-solve unknown words and are beginning to look at a word's initial consonant within a line of text.

_____ are beginning to grasp one-to-one matching and directionality (two lines of text).

_____ are aware of the difference between a letter and a word.

_____ can distinguish between text and illustrations.

_____ are active participants in reading the text during Shared Reading—make predictions, comprehend text, retell stories, and engage in class discussions.

_____ when writing, are beginning to articulate words slowly and record initial and final consonant sounds.

Reading and Writing in Kindergarten   Scholastic Professional Books

Guided Reading Planner

Date: _____   Group: _____

Title of book: _____

Level: _____

Focus: _____

Planning

Significant Words: _____

Discussion Questions: _____

_____

_____

_____

_____

Word Study: _____

_____

Student's Name	Observations	Teaching Points

Reading and Writing in Kindergarten Scholastic Professional Books

Guided Reading Booklist

Group: _____

Date	Title	Level

Reading and Writing in Kindergarten   Scholastic Professional Books

Chapter Five

Read Aloud for Fun and Excitement

Read-Aloud is when students gather together and listen to their teacher read all sorts of texts and stories they wouldn't be exposed to otherwise. The literature, chosen because it's rich and meaningful, is beyond the children's ability to read on their own or in Shared and Guided Reading. Read-Aloud plays an effective and important role in a comprehensive literacy program. Children love it, and hearing wonderful stories and poems is highly motivational.

Read-Aloud opens children up to the excitement and powerful language of the world of literature. It gives them the chance to:

◆ experience a variety of texts and genres and thus realize the benefits of knowing how to read.

◆ have conversations about books—listening and responding to one another's comments. Such "accountable" talk will be a useful tool for learning in math, science, and social studies.

◆ hear fluent and expressive reading that illustrates how words can create pictures
in their minds.

By encouraging a natural and purposeful use of oral language, you are furthering
the development of literacy skills as described by such oral language/literacy theorists
as Judith Newman and Brian Cambourne.

In my kindergarten class, Read-Aloud may happen a number of times during
the day. I have a set time each day when I read a specific chapter book, one of a
series of books about the same character, a book written by an author that the class
is studying, or a book that relates to the genre we're studying. Sometimes, however,
Read-Aloud can happen spontaneously when the time is right—when a poem or
story fits something that comes up in the classroom or when we need a calming
influence during a hectic day. I also make time to read a picture book each day.

GETTING READY TO READ ALOUD

Before I read to the class, I study and prepare the text. I go through the story and
plan all of the questions that I'm going to ask as I read. I write these on sticky notes
and put them right on the places where I intend to stop and ask the question.

I also select words that I will ask children to define for me. They quickly
learn that you can figure out the meaning of an unfamiliar word by reading the
words or sentences surrounding it. What a powerful technique for increasing
children's vocabulary it is—teaching them the meanings of many new words in
context instead of in isolation. I make a point of trying to use the new words we
learned during a Read-Aloud throughout that same day and beyond. For example,
if we learned the word *contented*, later in the day I might say, "Seeing you work so
hard during Reading Station time made me so.o..o...o contented." I insert the
words playfully at appropriate times, and children often respond with "That's the
word we learned," through their laughter. Then they use the word themselves when
they see an opportunity. This game is fun and helps students add new words to
their vocabulary.

Skill-Building Questions for Read-Aloud

The questions to ask children during Read-Aloud should require them to:

* recall details.
* make inferences.
* check predictions and support them with evidence.
* discuss problems and solutions.
* identify settings.

* describe characters.
* make personal connections.
* make connections to other books they've read.
* state opinions.
* discuss questions or confusions.
* retell the events in the story.

If I'm reading a book that takes more than one day, I start the next session by having the children recap what happened in the previous session. I ask them to support their answers with evidence from the text just as they do for Shared and Guided Reading.

START DISCUSSIONS

During a Read-Aloud, I promote comprehension by stopping at certain places to discuss aspects of the book. I continually model ways to discuss books. The students become familiar with such phrases as:

* This reminds me of . . .
* I don't understand . . .
* I think . . .
* I wonder why . . .
* This is like the book . . .

* I know . . .
* It was cool when . . .
* I agree . . .
* I disagree . . .

The conversations I model during and after Read-Aloud help children talk about the books they read during Independent Reading (see Chapter Six). I encourage the students to express their thoughts or respond to questions by sharing with the whole class or by telling it to the person sitting beside them.

MAKING INFERENCES

It's important for children to become aware that there is specific information that they may not find in the text. I explain that they may have to search for clues or put together bits of information to figure out what the author means or what message he or she is trying to get across. During Read-Aloud discussions, I sometimes read a

passage or sentences from the book to promote inferential thinking. For instance, a sentence in Cynthia Rylant's *The First Book* reads, *Henry's heart hurt*, and I ask the children, "What do you think the author meant by that?" Children can respond that Henry is sad, even though the text doesn't explicitly say so. When the text reads, *He thought Mudge made everything safe*, children have to infer the reason.

VISUALIZING WHAT'S HAPPENING

Another simple, fun activity that enhances the children's understanding and connection to the story asks them to listen, visualize, and draw an image that the text creates in their mind. For example, a passage in *The First Book* reads, *One day Mudge took a walk without Henry. The sun was shining, the birds were flying, the grass smelled sweet.* I ask the children to think about what pictures the words create in their minds and then draw those pictures.

READ-ALOUD RESPONSES

When you read aloud, you want your students to listen and respond with their own ideas. Here are two activities that will support your students in making thoughtful responses.

❋ Response Handbook

As a class, create your own Read-Aloud handbook to keep track of all the books you've read to your students and the children's responses. I use an enlarged, blank Big Book or chart tablet for my book; see sample at right When I finish a Read-Aloud, I write down some information about it in the handbook. Each book has its own page, and on that page we include: a copy of the cover, the title, author, and the genre. Through determining the genre, the students learn the difference between fiction, nonfiction, poetry, and fairy tales.

A page from our Read-Aloud handbook

After we've read a book once, children respond orally, with an illustration, or in writing. However, I don't ask children to respond in written form until they've had plenty of experience responding orally and

through illustrations. Once they're ready, I choose one child to contribute a response (one page) to the handbook in written or illustrative form. Each child gets at least one opportunity to respond in the handbook during the year. Types of responses include:

- writing an opinion of book.
- telling about a favorite part.
- describing a favorite character.
- making personal connections.
- retelling the story.
- writing facts learned from nonfiction text.

I use a familiar Shared Reading Big Book to demonstrate each type of response before I add it to our list of possibilities. I introduce one type of response at a time. For example, we may discuss—and practice writing about—favorite parts of a story for a while. Once the children are comfortable with responding that way, I move on to another type. The students draw illustrations to match their words and share their responses with the class. They can work on these responses during Reading Play Stations time.

✸ Response Journal

When I'm reading series books to the class, I make a journal for children to respond in. When reading the series books *Henry and Mudge* by Cynthia Rylant, for example, I make a response journal out of a composition notebook. I decorate the cover with copies or drawings of the story's characters. I usually get a stuffed animal that represents one of the characters from the book. For *Henry and Mudge*, I get a stuffed dog to represent Mudge.

▲ I played with Mudge. I fed him a bone

Each day one child gets to take Mudge and the journal home. At home, children write about what they did with Mudge while he was with them. I always write the first entry as a model of what to do. My entry might be: *Yesterday Mudge and I ate dinner together just like Henry does. We ate pizza. Mudge loved pizza!* Children love this activity. They can't wait to be the one to take home the character. Some of the children's responses are shown at right.

STUDENT READ-ALOUDS

After hearing fluent and expressive reading, the students are eager to read aloud themselves. I give them plenty of opportunities. At this point, children and I develop a checklist of things to remember when they read aloud.

▲ I play helicopter with Mudge but Mudge was not doing nothing. He was just watching me. Mudge was not helping me with my homework. He was sleeping. Helicopter game was fun. We watched TV too. Mudge was fun!

Here are some of their ideas:

- ◆ Read like you talk.
- ◆ Use a loud voice.
- ◆ Look at the punctuation at the end of the sentence.
- ◆ Read with expression.
- ◆ Talk like the characters in the story.
- ◆ Show the pictures.

Children practice meeting the criteria of a good read-aloud in the Big Book Reading Play Station. After they've practiced reading aloud several Big Books, they choose one to read to the class. We may plan this for the end of the day. Many of us have uncomfortable memories from when we were made to read aloud or make oral presentations as students. If you keep this early experience entirely positive and supportive with no judgment or criticism from you or the rest of the class, you'll start children off on the right foot.

Great Read-Alouds for Kindergarten

Series Books

Cynthia Rylant
Henry and Mudge series (Aladdin)
Poppleton series
(Blue Sky Press)
Mr. Putter and Tabby series
(Harcourt Brace)

Arnold Lobel
Frog and Toad series
(Scholastic, Harper and Row)

James Van Leeuwen
Tales of Oliver Pig series
(Puffin)

James Marshall
George and Martha series
(Houghton Mifflin)

Edward Marshall
Fox series
(Dial Press)

Author Studies

Frank Asch
Bear's Bargain (Prentice Hall, 1985)
Bear Shadow (Simon & Schuster, 1983)

Goodbye House (Prentice Hall, 1986)
Mooncake (Simon & Schuster, 1983)
Skyfire (Scholastic, 1984)

Donald Crews
(all Scholastic)
Flying (1986)
Freight Train (1978)
Night at the Fair (1997)
Sail Away (1995)
School Bus (1984)
Ten Black Dots (1986)

Eric Carle
The Grouchy Ladybug
(Harper Collins, 1977)
The Mixed Up Chameleon
(Harper & Row, 1975)
Roosters Off to See the World
(Scholastic, 1972)
The Secret Birthday Message
(Harper & Row, 1986)
The Very Busy Spider
(Scholastic, 1984)
The Very Hungry Caterpillar
(Philomel, 1987)
The Very Lonely Firefly
(Philomel, 1995)

Robert Munsch
(all Annick Press)
Andrew's Loose Tooth (1999)
Moira's Birthday (1989)
The Fire Station (1991)
Mortimer (1985)
Mud Puddle (1996)
Something Good (1990)
Stephanie's Ponytail (1996)
Thomas' Snowsuit (1985)

Ezra Jack Keats
Dreams (Macmillan, 1974)
Goggles (MacMillan, 1969)
Peter's Chair (Harper Collins, 1967)
The Snowy Day (Scholastic, 1962)
The Trip (Mulberry Books, 1978)
Whistle for Willie (Penguin Books, 1964)

Books that Promote Personal Connections
Alexander and the Horrible No Good Very Bad Day by Judith Viorst (Scholastic, 1972)
Amazing Grace by Mary Hoffman (Dial Books, 1991)

Birthday Presents by Cynthia Rylant (Orchard Books, 1987)

Chrysanthemum by Kevin Henkes (Greenwillow, 1991)

Corduroy by Don Freeman (Scholastic, 1968)

Harry the Dirty Dog by Gene Zion (Harper & Row, 1956)

I Know a Lady by Charlotte Zolotow (Puffin Books, 1984)

I Like Me! by Nancy Carlson (Puffin Books, 1990)

Ira Sleeps Over by Bernard Weber (Scholastic, 1972)

Just Grandpa and Me by Mercer Mayer (Paperwing Press, 1985)

Leo the Late Bloomer by Robert Krauss (Harper & Row, 1971)

Me Too! by Mercer Mayer (Houghton Mifflin, 1991)

Miss Nelson Is Missing by Harry Allard and James Marshall (Houghton Mifflin, 1977)

No David by David Shannon (Scholastic, 1998)

A Pocket for Corduroy by Don Freeman (Puffin, 1978)

Sheila Rae, The Brave by Kevin Henkes (Greenwillow, 1987)

The Tenth Good Thing About Barney by Judith Viorst (Macmillan, 1977)

There's a Nightmare In My Closet by Mercer Mayer (Dial Books, 1968)

There's Something In My Attic by Mercer Mayer (Dial Books, 1988)

Things I Like by Anthony Browne (Houghton Mifflin, 1991)

Today Was a Terrible Day by Patricia Reilly Giff (Puffin, 1980)

When I Was Five by Arthur Howard (Harcourt Brace, 1996)

When I Was Little by Jamie Lee Curtis (Harper Collins, 1993)

Will I Have a Friend? by Miriam Cohen (Macmillan, 1967)

William's Doll by Charlotte Zolotow (Harper & Row, 1972)

Books About Family

Guess How Much I Love You by Sam McBratney (Candlewick Press, 1994)

I Love My Sister (Most of the Time) by Elaine Edelman (Puffin, 1984)

I'll Fix Anthony by Judith Viorst (Aladdin Paperbacks)

Koala Lou by Mem Fox (Harcourt Brace, 1988)

Little Nino's Pizzeria by Karen Barbour (Harcourt Brace, 1987)

More, More, More Said the Baby by Vera B. Williams (Greenwillow, 1990)

My Dad Is Awesome by Nick Butterworth (Candlewick Press, 1989)

Noisy Nora by Rosemary Wells (Scholastic, 1973)

The Relatives Came by Cynthia Rylant (Simon & Schuster, 1985)

The Terrible Thing That Happened At Our House by Marge Blaine (Scholastic, 1975)

The Trouble With Mom by Babette Cole (Putnam & Grosset, 1983)

Watch Out For Chicken Feet In Your Soup by Tomie de Paola (Simon & Schuster, 1974)

Books About Friendships

Best Friends by Miriam Cohen (Macmillan, 1971)

Chester's Way by Kevin Henkes (Greenwillow, 1988)

Follow the Moon by Sarah Weeks (Harper Collins, 1995)

The Knight and the Dragon by Tomie de Paola (G.P. Putnam, 1980)

Rainbow Fish by Marcus Pfister (North-South Books, 1992)

Rosie and Michael by Judith Viorst (Aladdin, 1988)

Swimmy by Leo Lionni (Random House, 1993)

Rhyming Books

Jillian Jiggs by Phoebe Gilman (Scholastic, 1985)

Madeline by Ludwig Bemelmans (Puffin, 1977)

Nicketty-Nacketty Noo-Noo-Noo by Joy Cowley (Mondo, 1996)

"Quack!" Said the Billy Goat by Charles Causley (Harper & Row, 1970)

Where Have You Been? by Margaret Wise Brown (Scholastic, 1984)

Chapter Six

Independent Reading to Reinforce Skills

Independent Reading time is an exciting part of each day. Children enjoy reading on their own, and you have the opportunity to see how they're transferring and internalizing all of the new knowledge that you've taught them during Shared and Guided Reading. Before each session, I conduct a brief mini-lesson for the whole class to reinforce a skill or strategy that's already been taught. Then, the students choose a book from their group's Independent Reading baskets. (Independent Reading groups are the same as the Guided Reading groups.) They read on their own or with a buddy for 10 to 20 minutes. During the sessions, I meet with individual students to assess their progress and their needs. Afterwards, the class and I gather together and reflect on our experiences.

PLANNING FOR INDEPENDENT READING

❋ Identifying the Books

It is crucial that children have Independent Reading books available to choose from that are on their level. The books are stored in special Independent Reading baskets. In September and October, before we begin Guided Reading, children read at their tables. The baskets are labeled according to the tables where children sit. There are two kinds of books in the baskets: smaller versions of the Big Books we've read during Shared Reading and other books with two words to a line per page.

In November, when children are assigned to Guided Reading groups, they work in those same groups for Independent Reading. Every group gets its own basket of about 25 Independent Reading books to choose from. These books should be at the same level as the books the group is reading during Guided Reading sessions. This enables teachers to see if children can read other books on the same level without assistance. If they can, they have truly mastered that particular Guided Reading level. It's also helpful to include some books that are one level below their level to promote fluency and phrasing and build confidence. I update the baskets as the group's needs change. In addition, students have the opportunity to visit the classroom library and browse weekly.

❋ Keeping Track of the Books

I make a chart for each group to keep track of the books children are reading independently. On one side is a list of all of the books in the group's Independent Reading basket with students' names listed across the top; see sample at right.

As I prepare and update the groups' book baskets, I write the titles of all the books that are in the basket on the record sheet. As students read the books, I put a checkmark and the date under their names. This helps me keep track of which children still need to read a book at a certain level and shows which books I'll need to remove from the basket. Whenever I put a new level of books in the basket, I write a new list. Another benefit to this system is that it gives the children a sense of accountability and

Independent-Reading Records

Group:

The Green House

Books/Level	Student Cassandra	Student Andrew	Student Paige	Student Gonzalo	Student Nina
I Like Balloons (A)	✓ 11/15	11/16 ✓			
Look! (A)					11/15 ✓
Ben's Red Car (A)		11/15 ✓			
To School (A)				11/15 ✓	
Mom (A)	✓ 11/16				
Life on A Farm (A)			11/15 ✓		
Playing (A)					11/16 ✓
A House (A)					
Look At Me (B)					
At the Zoo (B)					
The Long Long Tail (B)					
Ball Games (B)					
I Can Read (B)				11/16 ✓	
Ben's Red Car (B)					
Balloons (B)					

Independent Reading record-keeping form

98

achievement. They can quickly see which books they've read and which they still need to read. Each child chooses one book to take home after an Independent Reading session. In my class, I call the children table by table and stand by their cubbies as they tell me the name of their book. I place the date in the box that corresponds to their name. You'll surely come up with a tracking system of your own that suits your style and the set-up of your classroom.

INDEPENDENT READING MINI-LESSONS

Topics for the mini-lessons that I teach before each Independent Reading session are based on new skills I want to introduce and on my observations of students' reading behaviors during Shared, Guided, and Independent Reading. At the beginning of the year, many of the lessons are based on management issues. Later on, they focus more on skills and strategies.

During a mini-lesson, I demonstrate exactly what I want my students to do while they're reading on their own. For example, if I want them to cross-check meaning and visual cues by looking for known parts in words, I copy a page from a familiar book from Shared Reading and put it on a transparency sheet. I place the sheet on an overhead projector and read it to the class. As I'm reading the text, I *think aloud,* verbalizing my thought processes about how to figure out a word I don't know. By saying aloud what is usually an internalized process, I'm modeling a strategy, and I'm also sending a message to the independent reader that though the learning process may be a little scary, it *is* manageable if we think things through. Here's an example of how I think aloud to model the cross-checking strategy.

What I do: I read the following excerpt from the book *Shark In A Sack* by Joy Cowley, but I substitute the word *pot* for the word *pan.*
Can you put a hen in a hat?
Can you put a pig in a pot (pan)?

What I think (aloud): *I don't think that's right. It could make sense because there's a picture of a pot, but* (I point to the word *pan*) *that doesn't look like the word pot. If the word were pot, there'd be the ot chunk at the end, like in the quick-and-easy word* got *on our Word Wall.*

What I do: I write *got* on my wipe-off board, erase the *g*, put a *p* in its place and say *pot.*

What I think
(aloud):   *I know that word (pointing to* pan*) isn't* pot. *What do I know about it that can help me figure it out? Oh! I see the* an *chunk in it like in the word* can.

What I do: *I write the word* can *on my wipe-off board, erase the* c, *put a* p *in its place and say* pan. *I read* Can you put a pig in a pan?

What I think
(aloud):   *That makes sense. It sounds right and looks right.*

Ideas for Management Mini-Lessons

✴ Sitting in your seat with your basket of books

✴ Reading with inside voices

✴ Sharing the books with your group

✴ Putting away the reading baskets

✴ Choosing a book to take home and putting it in your cubby

Ideas for Skill and Strategy Mini-Lessons

✴ Handling books

✴ Turning pages

✴ Reviewing the front and back of the book

✴ Looking at the pictures to predict the text

✴ Reviewing directionality

✴ Matching words one-to-one

✴ Cross-checking picture cues with the initial letter of a word

✴ Promoting self-monitoring and self-correcting

✴ Integrating cue sources (meaning, structure, visual)

✴ Looking at known parts in words and problem-solving new words

✴ Rereading to clarify confusions

✴ Verbalizing problem-solving strategies

✴ Practicing fluency and phrasing

✴ Understanding the meaning of punctuation marks and use of speech bubbles

✴ Understanding that reading is meaningful

✴ Recognizing the features of different genres (fiction, nonfiction, poetry)

✴ Responding to the book (favorite part, retellings, personal connections, characters)

✴ Reading with buddies

If I want children to check to see if they understand what they're reading I demonstrate how to stop after reading a couple of pages, think aloud to themselves, and retell what's happened so far. I also model responding to texts by making personal connections, choosing favorite parts, and writing character descriptions. At the end of the mini-lesson, I send the students off to read independently.

ASSESSING INDEPENDENT READERS

Independent Reading is a great time to conference with students to observe and assess their reading behaviors and keep track of their progress. I meet with every student in my class at least once a week—five students a day. I use three approaches to assessment: an Assessment/Instruction chart to help plan future mini-lessons; a Running Record sheet to record specific reading behaviors for each child; and individual laminated Good Readers' Strategy Charts to provide support and self-assessment. I tailor my assessment to the needs of the particular child. I may take a detailed Running Record, listen to the child read and record observations on the Assessment/Instruction chart, or simply refer to the Good Readers' Strategy Chart with the child.

❋ Assessment/Instruction Chart

To create my assessment sheets, I divide a sheet of paper into three columns—one for the child's name and the date, one headed *Assessment* and one titled *Instruction*. As I listen to a child read, I jot down notes, which I use to plan future mini-lessons or Guided and Shared Reading sessions. If I see that a student is applying the strategy we've been working on, I have him model it for the class or his group. And I may point out the many strengths that the class has developed as a group of readers.

Name / Date	Assessment	Instruction
Jessica 2/16	Shark in A Sack Worked on fluency and Phrasing. Retold Story Very Well	Understanding the meaning and Use of Punctuation marks at the end of a sentence (Practice during Shared Reading)
Michael 2/16	Lazy Mary got Prompted Does that sound right? Asked child to write get the word got. ⓅIs that the word got? (Pointed to text)	Cross-Checking Structure with Visual Cues
Jane 2/16	To Town motorcycle/sc motor bike Making self-Corrections Rereading and Checking Meaning and visual cues.	Bring to class attention
Kelly 2/16	Kitty Cat and the Fish Prompted to look for known chunks in words - away Use Known word "day" to get to new	Prompt children to attend to and use visual information during shared reading and word "away" shared Writing.
Sage 2/16	I Like to Eat - Prompted to attend to print- one-to-one matching I like pizza I like to eat pizza	Demonstrate 1-1 Matching during Shared Reading. Reread Morning Messages and class News.

Independent Reading Assessment

❋ Running Records

Running Records, which provide detailed information as the child reads, help you identify your students' specific strengths and weaknesses. A Running Record allows you to record and analyze how the child handles each word as he or she reads the text. You can take a Running Record on a blank piece of paper, create a form for yourself, or use a published Running Record Sheet; see the sample below. For each line of text, you make a check for every word the child reads correctly. If the child makes an error, you simply write what the child said over what the text read For example, if a child reads *book* instead of *library*, you write *book/library*. This process give you a complete record of the child's reading, which you can then analyze to identify the reading strategies a student is using or neglecting. Special codes are used to represent how the student reads the text. Here are some of the codes I use:

◆ The child read the word correctly = ✓

◆ The child substitutes a word in place of the word written in the text = Child: <u>Meet</u>
Text: Most

◆ The child omits a word = <u>——</u>
table

◆ The child self-corrects herself = <u>kitten|SC</u>
cat |

◆ The child rereads a word or a portion of the text = R

Coding technique is described in greater detail in Marie Clay's *An Observation Survey of Early Literacy Achievement*, (Heinemann, 1993) and in Mary Shea's *Taking Running Records*, (Scholastic, 2000).

I begin by asking the child to read the book he's selected. At the beginning of the year, the books are short enough for the child to read the entire book at one sitting. But as the texts get longer, the child may read just part of the book. As she reads, the Running Record enables me to analyze the child's errors, or miscues, to see what strategies and cueing sources she is using effectively, and what kind of help she needs.

Running Record

Name: *Andre* Date: *11/13*

Text: *A*

Scores: Running Words *41* Error Rate: *1:10* Accuracy *90%* Self-Correction Rate: *1:*
Number of Errors *4*

Analysis: ☐ Easy 95-100% ☑ Instructional 90-94% ☐ Hard 50-89%

Meaning (M)
Structure (S)
Visual (V)

Using meaning cues (relying on pictures) need to work on one-to-one matching and cross-checking meaning with initial visual cues. Able to read and locate high frequency words.

Page	We Go Out	E	SC	E MSV	SC MSV
②	✓ ✓ ✓ ✓ books/library. We go to the	1		M	
④	✓ ✓ ✓ ✓ ✓ We go to the park.				
⑥	✓ ✓ ✓ ✓ ✓ We go to the pool.				
⑧	✓ ✓ ✓ ✓ field — We go to the soccer game.	1 1		MS	
⑩	✓ ✓ ✓ ✓ ✓ We go to the beach.				

Information Used

Analyzing Errors: When I analyze an error, I record the cueing sources that the child used. For example, if the child substituted the word *chickens* for *birds*, I code the error with an *M* and *S* for meaning and structure cues because the word did make sense in context and it sounded grammatically correct. I wouldn't code it as *V* for visual because the words *birds* and *chickens* don't look visually similar. This tells me that the child needs practice with visual cues.

✓	✓	✓	birds		Error
I	see	the	chickens		M S

Self-Correction: When I analyze a self-correction, I code the error first and then, to the right of the coded error, record the additional cue source that the child used to make the correction.

✓	✓	✓	puppy	sc	Error	sc
I	like	the	dog		M S	V

Analyzing Running Records gives me a chance to see how well the students are transferring the knowledge and skills I'm teaching in Guided and Shared Reading to their independent reading.

I record the total number of errors the child makes while reading in order to obtain a percentile rate, which indicates whether the text is at the child's easy, instructional (the child can read it with some assistance from the teacher), or difficult level. (These levels are often referred to as *independent, instructional* and *frustration levels.*) In *An Observation Survey of Early Literacy Achievement*, Marie Clay provides a chart to calculate each child's percentile by creating a ratio of the words read to the number of errors. If children are scoring 95% or higher on many of the books at a specific level, they've probably mastered that level. By analyzing the child's errors, or miscues, to discover what cue sources the child is using to figure out an unknown word, I can provide appropriate instruction and prompts. For example, if the child is only using meaning cues, I note that I should prompt her to use visual and structural cues as well.

André's Running Records Throughout the Year: Here is a progression of some of the running records that I took of kindergartner André's reading during the course of one school year. As the year progressed, he read increasingly difficult levels of text and used a variety of strategies.

Mid November: This running record is shown on page 102. Notice that André relies on meaning cues. For example, for the text *We go to the library*, he read *We go to the books*. He used a meaning cue as his source because the illustration had many books in it. The error doesn't sound right within the line of text and the word *books* doesn't look visually similar to the word *library*. On subsequent pages, André read *field* for *soccer*, *ducks* for *farm* and *fishes* for *aquarium*. André's

spoken words don't match the printed text, indicating André also needs practice with one-to-one matching. He read, *We go to the field.* The text said, *We go to the soccer game.*

Late February: A running record taken three months later shows that André is beginning to cross-check meaning cues with initial visual cues. Although the text says *Little Teddy went to look for a home*, he read *Little Teddy went to look for a house.* By substituting *house* for *home*, he used meaning and visual cues. *House* makes sense in the context of the story and it begins with the same letter as *home.*

At this point, André is also beginning to reread to clarify confusions and monitor what he's reading. For example, the text says *Where can I sleep?* André read *What can I sleep?* He reread the sentence and said, *That's not right!* He is mastering one-to-one matching and making self-corrections based on visual cues. In one session, at first he substituted *bunny* for *rabbit* and *dolls* for *people*, taking notice of meaning and structure cues. But when he reread the text, he made the corrections by paying attention to the visual cue. He realized that the words he had substituted didn't look like the words in the text.

Late March: As the year goes on, André is developing a bank of quick-and-easy words that he can read and write, and he has learned lots of new words. André does more self-monitoring and rereading when something doesn't sound right. He can self-correct by noticing chunks and using what he knows about one word to get to another word. For instance, when he first read the sentence, *The waves came up to Sally's bucket and they took it away*, he said, *The waves came up to Sally's bucket and they take it away.* But then he corrected himself, *Oh! That doesn't sound right. The word is* took *like the word* look. When he was figuring out the word *away* he said, *That's like the word* day; *it has the* ay *chunk.* And when he was figuring out the word *sand* he said, *That's the* and *chunk like in* hand. *It starts with an* s. *It's* sand.

By now André can make corrections by integrating all three cueing sources. For the text *Come back, little red bucket! She shouted*, he read, *Come back, little red bucket! She said.* His substitution made sense, sounded right, and looked visually similar. It had the same beginning letter and the same letter at the end. When making the correction, André read the *sh* digraph rather than reading the *s* in isolation. And he understood the use of the exclamation point.

Late April: Now, instead of just looking at the beginning of a word, André has learned to go across the entire word and look for known parts. When figuring out the word *swinging*, he said, sw *is like the word* sweater (referring to class chart) *and* ing *is like Irving's name* (pointing towards the Name Chart). *The word is* swinging.

Because André has gained an understanding of the meaning and use of punctuation marks, he can read more fluently with accurate phrasing. He reads in a questioning tone or in an excited voice when he sees question marks and exclamation points. He understands what he's reading and can retell the story.

As you looking at André's reading progress, you will notice that whatever he didn't know at first, he mastered later. Most of the kindergarteners I work with show similar progress. If children are given daily opportunities to read and write in a supportive environment and all of the instructional plans are based on the needs of the students, they grow dramatically in their literacy skills. Remember that it's essential to revisit strategies you've already taught as you teach new ones. Children need constant reinforcement and modeling.

Organizing Running Records: Kelly DeGulis, a teacher whom I worked with at P.S. 198, devised a simple, effective way to keep track of the running records she took in her classroom. She keeps them all in a one binder that includes a separate section for each child. At the front of the binder is a page that lists the students down the side and the current month at the top. Each month she adds a new page. Every time she takes a running record she records the date next to the child's name. This recording system keeps track of how many running records you've taken for each child that month and provides a quick overview so you know right away if a child hasn't had one taken in a while. You can also keep a yearly log, like the one shown above; see template on page 111.

Running Record Yearly Log

Name	Sept.	Oct.	Nov.	Dec.	Jan.	Feb.	Mar.	Apr.	May	June
Amber	18,27	18,30	9,30	5,19						
Lili	19,28	3,24	2,28	7,21						
Michael	20,26	12,26	14,29	4,18						
Emma	14,21	5,19	16,23	3,20						
Jonathan	13,24	2,23	19,27	10,21						
Carolina										

❋ Good Readers' Strategy Chart

Toward the middle of the year, I give each child his or her own laminated copy of the Good Readers' Strategy Chart (see page 20). The charts are placed in each group's Independent Reading basket. If, while a child is reading to me, I notice that he needs to work on one of the strategies listed on the chart, I pull out the chart and use highlighting tape to highlight that strategy. I remind the child to use that strategy when he's trying to figure out a word during Independent Reading. When I meet that child on another day, we refer to the chart and discuss how he used the strategy. I remove the tape and use it to highlight another strategy as the need arises. This technique reminds children what they need to work on as they read on their own.

TEACHER/STUDENT TALKS AFTER INDEPENDENT READING

After I take a running record or listen to a child read, we talk about what happened during the session. I always begin by praising and validating the strategies she used. Then I focus on one or two areas—areas that I feel she will gain the most from.

What's the Good News? (Positive Prompts)

★ That was so smart how you reread the sentence and then corrected yourself. You knew that the word _____ didn't look right or make sense!

★ I like how you checked the picture and the beginning of the word.

★ It's great that you're noticing the endings of words when you're reading.

★ Wow! I see how you're looking at chunks in words and parts of words when you're trying to figure out a new word.

★ You're always checking to see if what you read makes sense in the story. That's great!

★ I can tell that you're really thinking about what's happening in the story.

★ I love how you stopped and noticed that what you read didn't sound right.

★ It's wonderful how you correct yourself when you make a mistake! You're checking whether what you read makes sense, sounds right, and looks right.

★ I like how you pointed to each word to check and see if what you read matches the words on the page.

★ You read so smoothly like you were talking. That's great!

★ I like how you read with expression when you saw the exclamation mark at the end of the sentence.

★ What a great retelling of the story! You really understood what you read.

Then I point out her error, or miscue, and guide her to correct the error. Here are some examples of appropriate teaching points.

◆ On page _____ you said _____. Let's reread the sentence and check to see if it makes sense and sounds right.

◆ What would you expect to see at the beginning of the word _____?

◆ Does that look right?

◆ So when you're reading, it's important to check to see if what you said not only makes sense in the story but also looks like the word in the book.

◆ Do you know another word like that word? Look for parts in words to help you figure out the new word. Always check to make sure the word makes sense in the story.

◆ Looking at the pictures in the book before you read the story will help you understand what the story is going to be about. Then as you're reading, it's easier to think about what's happening in the story.

Adapted from *Guided Reading* by Irene C. Fountas and Gay Su Pinnell.

MORE INDEPENDENT READING IDEAS

✱ Book Tapes

Every day during Independent Reading, one group of children listens to tapes of one or two books at their appropriate reading level. On each tape (I make the recordings myself), I read the story twice and then ask some comprehension questions. I ask one question at a time, wait thirty seconds or so, and then say the answer to the question. When the children play the tape, they read along silently with my first reading, read along aloud with the second, and then say the answer to each question. Within the 30-second lapses on the tape, they find the part of the story where the question is answered and check their answer before they hear me say it. When they shut off the tape, they reread the story on their own and take the book home for the night.

✱ Buddy Reading

Once a week I have children read with partners during Independent Reading. They choose a buddy from their group and select a book from their basket. One of my Independent Reading mini-lessons focuses on how to read with a partner. I put a book on an overhead transparency so all of the students can see the text. As I read the book with a student teacher, a school aide, or a colleague, I show students how to sit beside each other and take turns reading. I model the following behaviors:

◆ As one person is reading, the other person listens carefully and follows along.

◆ If the reader makes a mistake, the partner doesn't say the word for her, but instead guides her to check her Good Readers' Strategy Chart to problem-solve the word. Possible prompts include rereading, looking at the words and pictures, or looking at parts within words.

◆ The partners read the book for a second time in unison to promote fluency and phrasing. After the second reading, they orally respond to the book. Each week I'll give the children a different way to respond depending on what we've been practicing during Read-Aloud. For example, I may ask children to make personal connections to the text, discuss favorite parts or characters, or retell the story.

❋ Teacher-Made Books

Occasionally some children aren't ready to move on to the next level even if they've read all of the published books for their level. They may need more practice reading books that have repetitive patterns and only two or three words on a page. If that's the case, I make my own books for that beginning level. It's easy if you use stickers of objects, people doing things, animals, food, and so on. I put a sticker on each page of a blank book made of typing paper divided into four sections and write text that matches the picture under it. For example, under a picture of a dog I might write: *The dog, A dog* or *I see the dog*, depending on what the child knows and what he needs to practice.

▲ *To make a book for students: Make copies of each page. Cut into four sections. Staple the pages together to form individual books.*

WHOLE-CLASS READING REFLECTIONS ★

After Independent Reading, I always have a share session during which children explain how they applied the day's mini-lesson focus to their own reading. I also ask them to share any problem-solving strategies they used. They go back to the exact page where they figured out a word and explain their thought process. Sometimes I ask a child whom I met with to tell the class what she learned during our session.

I've found that all the literacy modeling I do throughout the day in Shared Reading, Guided Reading, and Independent Reading makes a big difference in helping children become independent problem-solvers and good readers.

Independent Reading Records

Group: _____

Books/Level	Student	Student	Student	Student	Student

Independent Reading Assessment

Name/Date	Assessment	Instruction

Running Record Yearly Log

Name	Sept.	Oct.	Nov.	Dec.	Jan.	Feb.	Mar.	Apr.	May	June

Chapter Seven

Shared and Interactive Writing Help Early Writers Flourish

Shared and Interactive Writing provide children with the modeling and assistance that guides them toward writing independently in the same way that Shared and Guided Reading instruction guide them toward reading independently. During Shared Writing, children help me develop the text and problem-solve words, but I write the text. During Interactive Writing, children and I compose text together, creating ideas and taking turns holding the pen. Including Shared and Interactive Writing in the kindergarten literacy program gives children a head start, if not a great advantage, in developing solid writing skills they can use throughout school and life.

SHARED WRITING

During Shared Writing, children and I create the text together. I hold the pen and do all the writing while the children watch. I often think aloud, demonstrating the writing process and applying problem-solving strategies to specific words. The text for Shared Writing can come from any source, including personal experiences, class experiences, conversations, and current events. The daily Morning Message, which invites children to write in a fun, playful, and meaningful way, is a great Shared Writing lesson.

✳ Morning Message

The Morning Message, which stems from an event that each child can relate to and understand, is developed from personal or classroom experiences. For example, a child's birthday can become the message *Today is Timmy's birthday.* All children can relate to the birthday theme, and they eagerly participate in the joy of the event. Of course, you won't have a birthday in your classroom every day, but if you present more routine Morning Messages excitedly, you'll get the same enthusiastic results. Morning Messages that give children something to look forward to, such as, *This afternoon we'll read lots of books and sing silly songs* or *This morning we will do some reading, and after lunch we will draw pictures during art,* can get the children excited, too. You can also interest children in bits of news from the neighborhood, city, or world.

I usually plan the message in advance so I can focus on specific letters, words, and skills I want the children to practice. For example, if I'm working on a specific letter chunk with the class, I'll include a word in the message that contains that chunk. But I'm flexible. Sometimes, I base the message on something that happened that morning or on something a child is excited about sharing.

I start out by saying the Morning Message aloud to the children. Each child repeats the message and counts the number of words. Then I begin writing the message on the chart tablet. At the beginning of the year, I write the entire message. As the year goes on, the children volunteer to come up and write letters, words, or portions of words. They refer to the Word Wall and various charts for support. When the children begin to hold the pen and write the words, the activity becomes Interactive Writing.

✳ Word Study During a Shared Writing Morning Message

As I write the text during Shared Writing, I use a number of techniques to encourage children to problem-solve words. For one, I encourage children to

articulate the words slowly and notice the sounds and the parts of the words that comprise those sounds.

I also think aloud to call attention to the chunks within known words and use them to solve the new words that I am writing. I highlight the familiar chunks, digraphs, blends, and endings of words as I write the Morning Message on the chart tablet. As I do, I indicate and verbalize each group of letters and the sounds that they make. After I write a word from the message and highlight what I want children to focus on, I point it out to children. For example:

I write:	What I may point out to the children:
This aftern*oon* we will read lots of books and sing silly song*s*.	The letters *th* make the /th/ sound! Look at the letters *oon* in *afternoon*. They make the /oon/ chunk. Adding an *s* to the end of the word *song* shows that there is more than one.
On *Tuesday* we had a *short* day of scho*ol*.	Look at the word *Tuesday*. Why does it have a capital *T*? See the chunk /ay/ in *day*. The letters *sh* in *short* make the /sh/ sound. The letters *ool* make the /ool/ chunk!
I am so happ*y* because *today* we will go on a class *trip* to the *c*ircus.	The *y* in the word *happy* makes the /ee/ sound. The word *today* has two words in it: *to* and *day*. That means it's a compound word. The letters *tr* in *trip* make the /tr/ sound. See the letter *c* in *circus*. Sometimes the *c* makes the *s* sound.
In the morning we'll do some r*ea*ding and then after lun*ch* we will get to make pictures of each other in art.	Notice that the letters *ea* in *read* make the /ee/ sound. The *ch* in the word *lunch* makes the /ch/ sound like in *Charlie* and *check* (refer to the name and digraph charts).
Look at the new *sp*ot for our comput*er*!	The *sp* in the word *spot* makes the /sp/ sound. The *er* in the word *computer* makes the /er/ sound.

An incredible amount of teaching and learning occurs during this five-to-eight minute activity. Along with the rapid recognition of chunks, blends, digraphs, ending sounds, and words, the Shared Writing Morning Message teaches children about word spacing, punctuation, and directionality. Seeing me write the words helps children understand that words are, in fact, separated, and that sentences, when there is no more room on the page, return to the start of the next line (the return sweep). This approach also introduces directionality, the beginning and ending of a sentence, the number of sentences in a message, and the use of punctuation.

❋ Word Study in Shared Writing Throughout the Year

These writing samples are from MaryAnn Wainstock's classroom.

November

Children write some quick-and-easy words and beginning sounds. MaryAnn Wainstock points out that the highlighted *ch* in *children* makes the /ch/ sound, and the first *c* in circus makes the /s/ sound.

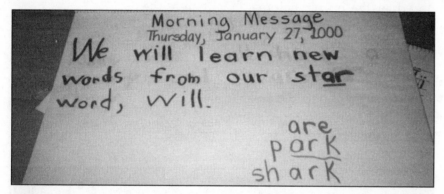

January

MaryAnn Wainstock helps children practice using known information about a word to get to a new word.

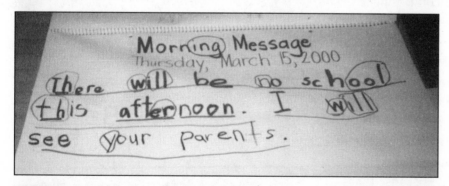

March

MaryAnn Wainstock highlights and discusses the chunks within the words *school* and *will* as well as the compound word *afternoon*, and the *th* digraph in *this* and *there*. She has children locate the separated sentences.

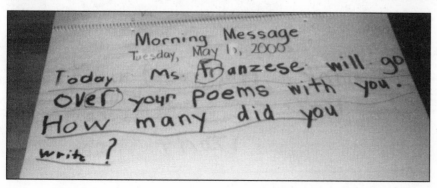

May

MaryAnn Wainstock has children identify the beginning and end of the two sentences. She and the children discuss the highlighted the *fr* blend and /er/ sound and the meaning and use of the question mark.

❊ Shared Writing Stories

For this technique, I read a story to the class and then tell them about a personal experience related to it. After telling about my personal experience, I draw a picture related to the story and my experience on the chart tablet. I then begin to write words under my picture.

For example, when I read *I Like* by Anthony Browne, I tell the class that I like to ride my bike in the park. I draw a picture on the chart tablet of a bicycle in a park. Then, one word at a time, I write my story. While I write the words, children recognize quick-and-easy words. Children and I practice saying the other words— stretching them out from beginning to middle to end. I sometimes refer to an alphabet chart to help children identify the sounds they hear. As children become better writers, I write my story and draw the picture before telling it since the children are now able to make meaning from the written words. Gradually children realize that stories are meaningful, well-organized, and purposeful.

Later on in the school year, I may write a personal experience story over a period of two or three days. Each day reread the story, and add details. I demonstrate how to insert information and check to see if the story makes sense and is clear. Though I am the scribe, the children are always actively engaged in the composing process. They offer suggestions and help me problem-solve unknown words. Just as I do during Interactive Writing, I demonstrate a variety of strategies for problem-solving words. I model the strategy on the practice page of the chart tablet where I'm writing the story. The top part of the chart tablet is the practice page and the bottom half is where I write the story. I model this format for the practice page because that's the way it will look in the children's journals; see example at right.

❊ Shared Writing Story Lesson

After I read the book *Little Nino's Pizzeria* by Karen Barbour to the class, I share details about how much my father loves to cook. Then I begin writing my story. (This takes about 20 minutes. If it seems as if it's going take longer, I pick it up the next day.)

Ms. Franzese: *How should I begin my story?*

Ricky: *My father loves to cook.*

Ms. Franzese: *That sounds like a good beginning, but I also want to add that he likes to cook a lot of things. How about,* My father loves to cook a lot of things. *I'll start with a capital letter because it's the beginning of the story.*

The first word of my sentence is My. My *is a quick-and-easy word from the word wall. Let's clap and chant the spelling of the word* My.

(We clap and chant *M* and *y*. I write the word *My* on the chart tablet.)

Ms. Franzese: *Great! Let me think about my story . . . What's the word that comes after* My . . .? (pointing to *My*)

Children: Father!

Ms. Franzese: *That's right!* Father! *It starts like . . .* fish. (I point to the alphabet chart.) *What is the first letter of* Father?

Children: F!

Ms. Franzese: *Right! Good!* F! (I write the *F*.) *What sound do you hear in the middle of the word* father? *It's like in* thumb. (I point to a chart that has a picture of a thumb with the digraph *th*.)

Jennifer: /th/, *th.*

Ms. Franzese: *That's right! Before the* /th/, *and after the* f, *there is an* a. (I write the *a*, go back to the *f*, place my finger under it, stretch and articulate the sounds as I move my finger across the word.) *Now, what do you hear at the end of the word? It's like in Amber's name.*

Amber: er!

Ms. Franzese: *Let me reread what I've written so far so I can get to my next word.* My father . . . *my next word is* loves.

Jonathan: *That's on the word wall.* Love *is a quick-and-easy word.*

(I write *love*)

Cassandra: *You need to put an* s *at the end of the word. It doesn't sound right.*

Ms. Franzese: *You're right.* (I reread to get to next word.) *My father loves . . .*

Children: To *is the next word.*

(The class enthusiastically spells *to* out loud.)

117

Ms. Franzese: *Great! Let's all go back and reread what I've written so far. My father loves to . . . cook. What do we know about the word* cook *that can help us spell it?*

Jason: *It sounds like* look. Look *is on the word wall.*

(I write *look* on the practice page.)

Ms. Franzese: *If I know* look *I can get to* cook. *I'll change the first part of the word* look *and keep the chunk* /ook/.
look   cook

Ms. Franzese: (I reread the text with the children.) *My father loves to cook a (I write the quick-and-easy word* a) . . . lot. *What word do I know on the word wall that can help me get to* lot?

Mary: Got.

Ms. Franzese: *Terrific. How can I get to the word* lot *using the word* got?

Mary: *Keep the chunk* /ot/ *and change the* g *to* l. (I show the work on the practice page as Mary explains it.)

Ms. Franzese: *That's wonderful. You really know how words work.* (I reread the text.) My father loves to cook a lot of . . .

Diamond: *Of's a quick-and- easy word from the word wall.*

(The children clap and chant spelling of the word *of* as I write it.)

Ms. Franzese: Things. *What do we know about that word?*

Jason: *It starts like* thumb *with the* /th/ *sound.*

Ms. Franzese: *That's right.* (I say word slowly with class.) Thing.

Emma: *I hear the* /ing/ *chunk at the end of the word.*

Ms. Franzese: *Yes! Since I'm finished with this thought, what should I do at the end of the sentence?*

Children: *Put a period!*

Ms. Franzese: *Right! When I was telling you the story, what did I say my father loved to cook?*

Lili: *Pasta with cheese.*

Ms. Franzese: *I want to add that to my story so that when you read it you can really get a picture in your mind of my father cooking. I want to write another sentence: He makes pasta with cheese on it. I'm going to start with a*

capital letter because it's the beginning of a new sentence. What's the first word of my sentence?

Alexandria: He.

Ms. Franzese: *What word can help me get to* he?

John: Me. *If you know* me *you can get to* he. (*I write the words* he *and* me *on practice page.*)
me
he

Ms. Franzese: (*I reread.*) He makes . . . *I'll say the word slowly and write down the sounds I hear.* (*The children say the word slowly with me*) /m/-/a/-/k/. (*I go across the word with my finger and record the letters that the children say. I write* mak). *Does that look right?*

Vanessa: *No.*

Ms. Franzese: *What's the silent letter we need at the end of the word to make it look right?*

Vanessa: e!

Ms. Franzese: *Great!* He make.

Eric: *That doesn't sound right. You need to add an s at the end.* Makes.

Ms. Franzese: (*I add the s and reread*) He makes . . . pasta. (*I write the word* pasta *as I say it slowly.*) *What's next?*

Jonathan: With! *It's a quick-and-easy word! We know how to write that word—* w-i-t-h!

Ms. Franzese: (*I reread.*) He makes pasta with . . . cheese. (*I say* cheese *slowly.*)

Jennifer: *It starts like* check–/ch/.

Ms. Franzese: *Right!* Ch! (*I write* ch.) *I'm going to run my fingers across the word, and let's say it slowly. What sounds do we hear?*

John: /e/ *and* /s/.

Ms. Franzese: *There are two e's in the middle of that word. There's a silent letter at the end of that word, what is it?*

Children: e!

Ms. Franzese: (*I reread:* He makes pasta with cheese. *I write* on *and* it *as I read since they are automatic, quick-and-easy words that the whole*

class knows.) I want to describe how it tastes. It's so good. What do you think I should write?

Vanessa: *It tastes so good.*

Amber: *It's delicious.*

Jonathan: *It is so yummy.*

Ms. Franzese: *All of those were such great suggestions, but I think I'm going to write* It is so yummy *because I always tell my Dad that his food is yummy. It's going to be a new sentence. How should I begin?*

Jennifer: *You have to begin the sentence with a capital letter.*

Ms. Franzese: It *and* is *are two quick-and-easy words. (I reread text:* It is.)

Jose: *The next word is* so.

Ms. Franzese: *What word can help me get to* so?

Jose: go.

Ms. Franzese: *(I write* go *on the practice page.)*

Jose: *Take away the first part of* go *and put an* s. *Keep the* o.

Ms. Franzese: *Good Job! (I reread:* It is so . . . yummy.) Yummy *starts like yo-yo. (I refer to class ABC chart.) What letter does it start with?*

Children: Y!

Ms. Franzese: *(I stretch out the word with the children /yu/) What's next? It's like umbrella. (I refer to the ABC chart.)*

Jennifer: u.

Ms. Franzese: Yumm. *What's next?*

Michael: *Like mailbox.* m.

Ms. Franzese: *Yes! There are two m's. What sound do you hear at the end of the word* yummy?

Kelly: *It's like in my name—Kelly! The* y *makes the* e *sound.*

Ms. Franzese: *Great!*

Kelly: *You should put an exclamation mark at the end of the sentence because you really love the pasta.*

Ms. Franzese: *That's right! Now let's reread the story to make sure that it looks right, sounds right, and makes sense.*

As with the reading process, I revise and direct my instruction based upon my observations of how the children are mastering skills. I use the Interactive and Shared Writing Skills checklist (see the reproducible on page 127) as a guide to determine what skills I need to cover during Interactive and Shared Writing instruction, and I continually refer to this checklist as the children begin to write independently.

INTERACTIVE WRITING

Interactive Writing gets kindergarten students involved in working with print and developing writing strategies right from the start. Together the children and I use wipe-off boards with markers, or chart tablets, or blank Big Books to compose text. We write every day during language-based activities such as Morning Messages, Class News, book retellings, class trips, letters, invitations, recipes, retellings, informational texts, class rules, and personal experience descriptions. We publish the output of many of these activities as class books, which students can revisit and reread. I use Interactive Writing with the whole class as well as in small group settings.

In my class, each child has his or her own personal wipe-off board and marker (Dorn, French, and Jones, 1998) to use for some Interactive Writing activities. The alphabet and name chart, word wall, blend/digraph chart, and chunking charts are displayed prominently, and we continually refer to them. At the beginning of the year the students write one line of text, but by spring they're writing two to four lines. Each lesson takes about 20 to 25 minutes.

Of course, at the beginning of the kindergarten year, children won't be able to compose all, or even a much, of a message or grasp all of the components of a written sentence. In fact, more often than not they know only certain letters or parts of words. My role is to help them write whatever part of the message they're capable of and to guide them to work on writing particular letters or words I'm concentrating on during reading lessons. I begin where they are and model what they haven't yet grasped in order to demonstrate what they'll eventually be able to do. I continually build on their present knowledge to help them acquire new skills.

The children and I share the pen using wipe-off boards during Class News throughout the year. Note the progression of skills in the following sequence.

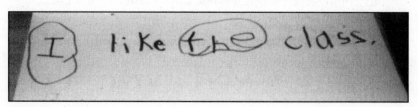

October

The child and teacher share the pen. The teacher writes the word *like*. The child writes the quick-and-easy word *the*.

121

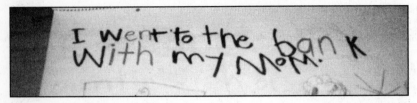

November

The teacher writes the middle and ending sounds of some words. The child writes more quick-and-easy words and beginning sounds on her own.

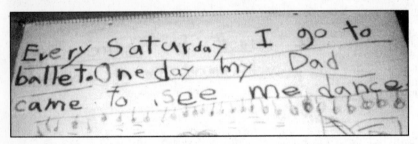

April

The student takes ownership of the pen and writes one sentence. She hears and records beginning, middle, and ending sounds of words.

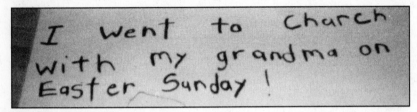

May

The student takes ownership of the pen and writes two sentences.

❋ The Benefits of Interactive Writing

Interactive Writing helps children absorb and understand early writing strategies and reinforces their sense of how words work. It gives them the chance to realize the power of producing meaningful text. As we write together, children quickly learn such early print concepts as directional movement and one-to-one matching. They gain a strong sense of letter-sound correspondence, and they also learn to form letters accurately, write a variety of quick-and-easy words, and notice specific features within letters and words. They come to understand the use and meaning of punctuation marks. They also learn to proofread their work to make sure the text makes sense, sounds right, and looks right. Most important, Interactive Writing is another way the children become active problem-solvers.

❋ A Beginning-of-the-Year Interactive Writing Lesson

During a brief class discussion before a Class News writing session, I single out Paige, and ask if she can think of something she'd like to write about. She tells me that she and her mom went to the bank yesterday. I have her come to the front of our meeting area to serve as the day's writer. The other students are ready to write on their wipe-off boards. Here's how the session went:

Ms. Franzese: *Paige, tell us the Class News message you want to write.*

Paige: *I want to write,* I went to the bank with my mom.

Ms. Franzese: *Let's say Paige's message all together.*

Children: I went to the bank with my mom.

Ms. Franzese: *Let's picture Paige at the bank with her mother. Close your eyes and try to see Paige and her mom in your mind. Now repeat the message again.*

Children: I went to the bank with my mom.

Ms. Franzese: *Can you count the number of words in the message? How many words do you count?*

Children: (Using their fingers, the children count.) *Eight.*

Ms. Franzese: *Good. Now we're ready to begin writing. We'll start with a capital letter because it's the first word of the sentence. (Later in the year, I'd ask the children to tell me how we should begin the sentence.)*

Ms. Franzese: *What's the first word of the message?*

Children: I.

Ms. Franzese: *Oh! That's a quick-and-easy word we already know how to write! Now, Paige, write the word I on the chart tablet. The rest of you write it on your wipe-off boards. (I want each child to go through the process rather than copy off of the chart tablet. If I need to, I may model how to form an I by verbalizing the movements I make as I write it.)*

Ms. Franzese: *Paige, now point to the word and everybody read it.*

Children: I.

Ms. Franzese: *What is the next word of the message?*

Children: Went!

Ms. Franzese: *What letter would you expect to see at the beginning of the word went? It's like* window. *(I point to the alphabet chart.)*

Children: w!

Ms. Franzese: *Let's write w. Be sure to leave a space after the word I before the w. It's important to leave spaces between words so it's easy to read them. (The children write w.)*

Ms. Franzese: *Now point to the letter* w *and say the word* went *slowly as you move your finger across the paper where the rest of the word will go. What do you hear as you say the word?*

Children: n.

Ms. Franzese: *There's also an* e *before the* n. (I write e on the chart tablet. At this point in the year, I don't ask the children to write the letters they don't come up with on their own. I want them to write just the words or parts of words they already know, and I support them by filling in what they don't yet know.)

Ms. Franzese: *Say the word* went *again slowly and tell me what you hear at the end of the word.*

Children: *The letter* t!

Ms. Franzese: *Yes. Let's write the letter* t. (I'm not really expecting the children to write with directionality or appropriate placement at this point. Instead, I want them to focus on early-writing skills, such as letter-sound correspondence, identification, and formation of familiar letters and words, and rereading to predict.)

After the children have written the entire message, I teach or reinforce some other skills. For example:

▲ *Children working with wipe-off boards during class news.*

◆ **To reinforce one-to-one matching:** I have the whole class read the message as the chart writer points to the words.

◆ **To provide practice with distinguishing various features of letter:** I ask the children to locate specific letters within the message. For Paige's message, I might ask for the letter that has sticks and slants (*k*) or a letter that has a circle and a stick (*b*).

◆ **To encourage children to use pictures as a source of information when they read:** I have the child at the chart tablet draw a picture of the message. For example, for

Paige's message, *I went to the bank with my mom*, the child might draw a picture of herself and her mom, the bank, or any combination of those images.

Each child's Class News message becomes part of a chart tablet book. I make sure each message is written correctly with standard spelling and letter formation. If the child at the chart tablet makes any mistakes, I cover them with correction tape and support the child in correcting them. I keep the Class News book in an accessible spot in the room so the children can practice rereading past messages.

✳ More Word Study

There are countless teaching opportunities you can use after children have completed an Interactive Writing message. Some of the things we do in my class include counting the number of sentences and words in the message and picking out compound words, contractions, endings, new words, high-frequency words, words with special spelling patterns, and consonant clusters (McCarrier, Pinnell and Fountas, 2000).

We also verbalize any problem-solving strategies already taught. I may ask the children to review how they went about using the chunk of a known word to get to a new word. And I may ask them to underline or circle specific quick-and-easy words or words that contain certain letter clusters.

Many other word-study skills can be addressed during an Interactive Writing session. For example, in the Class News message, *I went to the mall with my Dad to buy some shirts*, children practiced writing the quick-and-easy words *I, went, to, the, my*. When they problem-solved the words *mall* and *some*, they used the chunk *all* to get to *mall* and the word *come* to get to *some*. They referred to the name chart and digraph chart when writing the *th* in *with* and the *sh* in *shirts*. We also discussed the difference between the words *by* and *buy*.

With another Class News message, *My mother is going to have a baby on my birthday. It is going to be a girl*, the children and I:

◆ wrote the word *going* and discussed the *ing* at the end of the word.

◆ wrote the word *birthday*, articulated the word slowly from beginning to middle to end and wrote the known parts of the word.

◆ pointed out that the word *birthday* is a compound word.

✳✳ Classroom Hint

Set Aside Practice Places

As your students gain writing skills and learn to write their entire message with proper directionality and spacing, use the *practice-page* technique (*An Observation Survey of Early Literacy Achievement* by Marie Clay, 1993, and *Apprenticeship in Literacy* by Linda Dorn, Tammy French, and Cathy Jones, 1998). Practice pages are simply workspaces at the bottom of the wipe-off boards. The children use the space to practice forming letters and figure out words they don't know.

- used the known word *me* to get to the word *be*.

- talked about how the word *baby* had the *y* at the end just like the name of their classmate Kelly.

- discussed the number of sentences in the message, underlined each sentence, and reinforced that new sentences start with a capital letter.

❋ Other Interactive Writing Ideas

Class News is just one example of all the ways I integrate Interactive Writing into our literacy program. As I mentioned above, a world of possibilities exists.

Retelling: After the children saw a performance of the *Nutcracker*, we used Interactive Writing to retell the story. First the children retold the story orally. Then we shared the pen to compose their text. Since I wanted the children to practice new words—not ones they already knew—I had various children come up and write specific letters and words that they needed to practice. I wrote only the words they knew for them. I asked children who weren't at the chart to verbalize the movements as they formed the letter with their finger on the carpet.

▲ *MaryAnn Wainstock's kindergarten class retold the story of the* Nutcracker *for Interactive Writing. The children worked in groups to draw illustrations to match the text. It is important to discuss with children about what they're actually going to draw. You want them to understand that their pictures have to tell the same story the text tells.*

Class Stars: Each week MaryAnn Wainstock, one of the kindergarten teachers I worked with, chooses a different child to be a class star. As a class, the students list positive things about that child. For example, for John: *John is nice to everyone. John is a good reader and writer. John has a great smile.* MaryAnn posts the finished list outside of her classroom beside a baby picture and recent photo of the child, along with one of his or her published pieces of writing. Not only

▲ *In MaryAnn Wainstock's kindergarten, children write about a Class Star each week for Interactive Writing.*

are the children learning early writing strategies, but they are building their self-esteem as well.

Getting-to-Know-You Wall. Katherine Schnied makes a "getting to know you wall" at the beginning of the school year. Using Interactive Writing, children write about what they like to do. Katherine photocopies a picture of each child and puts it next to his or her work.

Shared and Interactive Writing Skills Checklist

Does the child . . .

____ recognize upper- and lower-case letters?

____ associate letters of the alphabet with their sounds?

____ understand that words are made up of letters and know the difference between a letter and a word?

____ recognize initial and final letters of words?

____ articulate words slowly and record sounds by letter representation?

____ understand one-to-one matching and left-to-right and top-to-bottom directionality?

____ use spaces between words?

____ identify and write some high-frequency words: *a, at, an, and, am, can, do, go, he, in, I, is, it, like, me, my, no, see, she, so, the, to, up,* and *we* (and his name)?

____ understand the meaning and use of punctuation?

____ problem-solve words by using what he knows about a word to figure out new words?

____ write letters in correct form and identify the distinctive features among letters?

____ link words to students' names?

Adapted from *Word Matters: Teaching Phonics and Spelling in the Reading/Writing Classroom,* Pinnell & Fountas (1998).

▲ *Geting-to-know-you wall*

Chapter Eight

Independent Writing Makes Them Proud

Children love to discover the connections between what they have learned in Shared, Guided and Independent Reading, and Shared and Interactive Writing. It's exciting for them to see it all come together in a meaningful context as they apply their knowledge and see themselves as successful readers and writers. It's a very powerful experience when children combine all the skills they're learning during Independent Writing.

THE WRITING ROUTINE

I have my students write independently every day. They write personal stories (one or two lines at the beginning of the year), nonfiction informational

articles, how-to descriptions, poems, letters, and more. Before each Independent Writing lesson, I conduct a mini-lesson based on my observations of the children's needs. And whenever I introduce a new type or genre of writing, I model the process to get the children started. After the lesson is over, we share the children's stories and insights, as well as reinforce skills and strategies again and again. The work of Lucy Calkins has provided a great deal of information on the subject of independent writing.

❋ Independent Writing Materials and Formats

The students write independently in journals and on prepared writing sheets that I format in advance.

Journals

I make writing journals with sheets of typing paper that I either bind with a binding machine or staple together (or you can buy unlined journals). One page of the journal spread is where the children write their stories. The other page of the spread serves as a practice page (adapted from *An Observation Survey of Early Literacy Achievement by Marie Clay, 1993,* and *Apprenticeship in Literacy* by Linda Dorn, Tammy French, and Cathy Jones, 1998). The practice-page technique provides the students with a space to practice writing words to see if they look right and to help them use known words to spell new words. As the children become used to figuring out words, they begin to internalize the process and don't use the practice page as often. This technique is first demonstrated during Shared Writing Stories (see page 116).

At the beginning of the year, children are just learning how to articulate words slowly and record the sounds they hear. They represent the pictures they draw with random strings of letters or with one or two letters that represent a word. So I start students off with journals that don't contain lines. Once I feel the children are able to write in-between lines, I put in lines and leave space for illustrations.

Classroom Hint

Explaining Trial and Error and When to Right Wrongs

In the kindergarten classroom—the first formal setting of a writer's life—it's especially important to balance the "correctness" of a young child's writing with the expectation of what he will be able to accomplish. When children write independently, they need a supportive, non-threatening environment so they can work without feeling like what they put down might be "wrong." Unlike in reading, a mechanical "mistake" during writing stays on the paper and can be frustrating and disruptive to the creative and purposeful aspect of writing.

I constantly encourage children to try out new strategies to figure out words and to accept that this often leads to mistakes—"trial and error." I explain that if we never try things out and risk making mistakes, we're unlikely to learn new things. My students understand that trial and error is a good thing. I use the practice-page technique (see page 116) to provide space for experimentation.

Generally, the topics for these journals are open-ended. If a child can't come up with a topic to write about, I brainstorm with him to find a topic based on his personal life and interests. I jot down the date on each journal entry to assess progress.

Special Paper

Sometimes I give the children specific types of paper to write on depending on the purpose of the assignment. For example, if they're writing how-to pieces (see page 139), which describe step-by-step procedures on how to complete a specific task, I might provide paper with appropriate boxes and lines. If children are keeping a log of their observations for a science activity, I might make individual booklets. Or if they're doing nonfiction writing, I give them a Facts-About sheet with lines. Using different types of paper and formats for different writing experiences shows children that there are varied mediums.

I always have children use pens to write words (and markers and crayons to illustrate) because I want to see their errors and use them to inform my teaching. I show children how to cross out any unnecessary words or information if they want to make a change.

MINI-LESSONS TARGETED TO WRITING SKILLS

I base my mini-lesson topics for writing on my observations during recent writing sessions and my assessment of past writing samples. In addition to modeling all the skills and techniques with my own writing during mini-lessons, I use writing from published authors to illustrate the kinds of things I want the children to do in their own writing. Most important, I use the children's pieces as teaching tools. For example, if a child used a technique that I demonstrated to the class, I share that. Or if I notice that my students need to work on a particular skill—such as adding more information to their writing—I take a student writing sample and show where adding more detail or descriptive words might make it better. Because I showcase the children's work in a positive and non-threatening way, they are very excited to be chosen to demonstrate their pieces and have them used as models. The students in my classroom know that we are partners in using all sources to learn together.

Writing-Skill Mini-Lesson Topics

Revision
Rereading text to see if the story makes sense
Adding information
Staying on one topic
Sequencing the events of a story
Endings
Choosing an appropriate title

Editing
Using upper- and lower-case letters appropriately
Spacing between words
Directionality
Awareness of end-of-sentence punctuation
   (period, question mark, exclamation point)
Correct formation of letters

Articulation
Saying words slowly to represent and record their sounds
Referencing the alphabet chart
Referencing the word wall
Using the practice page to figure out unknown words
Crossing out unnecessary letters or words that don't look right or sound right

✺ Sample Revision Mini-Lesson—Adding Information

When I notice that many children are writing good one-line pieces, such as *I love the snow. I like flowers. I love my Mom*, I know they are ready to work on adding more. I select Andrew's sentence, *I love the snow*, from his Independent Writing Journal and write it on a chart tablet. I copy everything exactly as Andrew wrote it, except that I correct any spelling errors and subtlety add punctuation as we become engaged in adding content details. Even though the purpose of the lesson is to add more content information to the writing, I want children to see conventional spelling and punctuation, especially when we're working together as a whole class. I feel it is better that children don't see teachers modeling incorrect spelling, and I don't want them to focus on words that don't look right. (Sometimes I type and enlarge the sample. If the sample is more than one line long, I leave two or three spaces between each line for added information.) Here's how our session went:

Ms. Franzese: *Andrew, I like how you began your piece. I love the snow, too. May I use it to help everyone in the class become better writers?*

Andrew: *Yes. Okay.*

Ms. Franzese: *Would you read your piece for the class?*

Andrew: *I love the snow.*

Ms. Franzese: *I was wondering, why do you love the snow?*

Andrew: *It's pretty and you can play in it.*

Ms. Franzese: *What do you do in the snow?*

Andrew: *I jump in it.*

Jonathan: *I make snow angels.*

131

Jason: *I throw snowballs.*

Ms. Franzese: *There are so many things that you can do in the snow. So what's one thing that you can add to your story?*

Andrew: *I jump in it.*

Ms. Franzese: *Let's write that on the chart tablet.*

(Andrew writes in front of the children. Children say the words slowly as Andrew records the sounds with their appropriate letters and writes the quick-and-easy words. I write some of the words as needed.)

Ms. Franzese: *What else can you add to your story to let us know why you like the snow so much? Let's try to use words that will help us get a picture of you in the snow.*

Mary: *He can write that he makes snow angels.*

Andrew: *I could write: I look out the window and see the snow.*

Ms. Franzese: *That would be a great thing to add. I can just see you looking out the window and watching the snow fall. When you go back to your journal, you can add this new information to your story.*

Today I want all of you to go back to your stories and reread them. Then add some more information to your piece just the way Andrew did.

Andrew's original journal entry:

▲ I love the snow.

Andrew's revision:

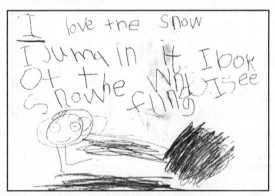

▲ I love the snow. I jump in it. I look out the window. I see snow falling.

Adding Information

Andrew's writing about the snow shows how students can apply the technique of adding important information to make their stories more meaningful. I share writing samples like this with the class because they show how to transfer new knowledge to their own work.

Not long after I held a mini-lesson on adding information, I observed Jane and Michael having a conversation during Independent Writing. Jane was reading her piece to Michael.

Jane: I will go to Florida in the summer. My sister can't come because she was bad. I will see my grandpa and grandma.

Michael: *Why was your sister bad? What did she do?*

Jane: *My mom told her to go to bed, and she said no.*

Michael: *You should add that to your story.*

Jane: *I will.*

Jane's initial piece:

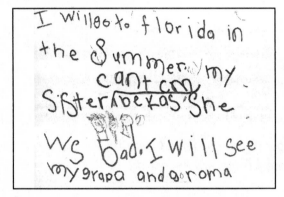

▲ I will go to Florida in the summer. My sister can't come because she was bad. I will see my grandpa and grandma.

What she added:

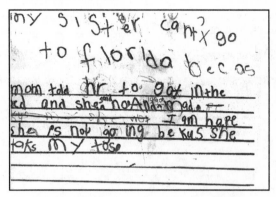

▲ My sister can't go to Florida because mom told her to go to bed and she said no. And she got mad. I am happy she is not going because she takes my toys.

It was wonderful to see Jane and Michael learning from each other and to see that they had transferred what they'd learned from our lessons to their own writing. They were beginning to understand that it's important to add information to clarify confusions and make writing more interesting. I repeated my Adding Information mini-lesson the next day to reinforce the concept by having Jane and Michael share their process.

MODELING WRITING

Before children write independently, I do a lot of modeling. I model exactly how to approach each type of writing. I begin by modeling an example of my own. Then before children begin writing their pieces, I have them tell me what they're going to

write so I can steer them in the right direction if they need help. At the beginning of the year, I repeat each word a child tells me as I point to a blank space on her journal page to show where she should write it. This pointing helps children visualize the words on the page and reinforces directionality. I encourage them to refer to the various charts around the room and their smaller versions of the classroom alphabet chart while they're writing.

I don't have the children use practice pages (see page 117) at the beginning of the year. I want them first to see me use them during Shared Writing and then work using them together with me during Interactive Writing. Over time, children begin to use the practice pages, but toward the end of the year they need to use them less often. As one student said to me at the end of the school year, "My practice page is blank because I can do it in my head."

Journal Pages with Their Practice Pages

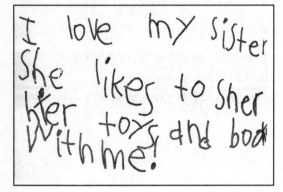

▲ I love my sister. She likes to share her toys and books with me.

▲ *Mary used the known word* boy *to get to* toy. *She used* me *to get to* she *and* look *to get to* book.

Writing my own stories in pieces in front of the children can serve as a mini-lesson. Sometimes I write a different part of a story each day, so that children understand that writing is a continuous process. A piece does not have to be finished in one day. The students learn that a writer goes back, rereads what she has written, and changes and adds to her story. Whatever I want my students to do in their writing, I model in my own writing.

For example, I model writing a personal story—the kind of writing we do most often—by first telling children the story I'm going to write. I tell it in a conversational tone using natural language. As I'm writing, I involve children in composing it with me. I ask them to suggest ways to begin my story or have them help me add details or events to add meaning. As I write the words, I ask them to help me problem-solve, and I demonstrate appropriate strategies. They articulate words slowly with me and

tell me what sounds they hear. I refer to name charts, alphabet charts, and blend/digraph charts as I record parts of words, and I refer to the word wall when I write quick-and-easy words. I illustrate how to use the practice page to form letters, write a word to be sure that it looks right, and use chunks to get to an unknown word.

WRITING CHATS

After I've presented a mini-lesson and/or modeled how to write a specific type of writing, children begin to write their own pieces. While they write independently, I move around the room and engage several children in quick individual conversations to support them in becoming better writers. During these "chats," I guide students in transferring mini-lesson skills to their own writing, so that later they'll understand how to apply them in their independent efforts. I make a point to end a chat by asking a child to try a specific strategy to the rest of his writing that day. For example, if I remind Mary how to articulate slowly and listen for sounds in sequence, I ask her to write the rest of the sentence using that strategy. At the end of writing time, I make sure that I go over to the students I've chatted with that day and check to see how they implemented their strategies. I always praise what each child has written as well as any problem-solving strategies they tried.

During an Independent Writing chats, I help my students by asking them to:

◆ talk about their experiences so they can choose a topic to write about.

◆ tell me the story out loud to figure out how they should begin the piece.

◆ reread the story to see if it makes sense and if the written text matches their spoken words.

◆ add more information to the story to clarify confusions or add meaning.

◆ cross out unnecessary words.

◆ say words slowly (beginning, middle, and ending sounds) to figure out words they don't know and write the appropriate letters.

◆ spell words by using chunking (working on the practice page).

◆ listen for parts in words.

◆ tell the events of the story to be sure they're in the right order.

◆ add an ending to their story.

◆ choose a title that describes the story.

Words That Say "You Are a Good Writer!"

* What a wonderful story you wrote! I could picture the story in my mind.

* I like how you added all of those important details to your story!

* Look at how you used a word you knew to get to a new word you wanted for your story!

* What good spacing between your words!

* I love your story's ending!

* The title you chose really describes your story.

* It's great how you stretched out your words and wrote down the beginning, middle, and ending sounds!

* I like how you put an exclamation mark at the end of that sentence. It shows me that you were excited.

* It was really smart of you to cross out the word _____ . It doesn't sound right to me either.

* You really know how to reread to figure out that next word!

SHARE TIME

Sharing stories and seeing each other's progress is an important part of literacy instruction for children. At the end of each writing session, gather the children together and choose two children to share what they've written. In my class, sometimes I'll choose a child who applied what I taught during a mini-lesson, or I select someone who tried something new. Children share completed stories and stories that need more information. I also ask children to tell us how they used their practice page and what problem-solving strategies they used to get to unknown words. The rest of the children tell what they liked about the piece and ask any questions they may have. I model appropriate responses to children's writing. Children generally make such comments as:

◆ I like how your pictures matched your words.

◆ I like the ending of your story.

◆ I like how you stretched out the words and wrote all of the letters.

◆ I like how you used the practice page.

◆ I like how you just wrote about one thing.

◆ I liked the part when you said_____.

◆ I have a question. (The children ask questions about the content of the story and suggest new information that the author can add to his/her piece.)

◆ I don't understand _____.

◆ I think you should add _____.

◆ Your story reminds me of when I _____.

Children learn a great deal from talking about the writing during share sessions.

KEEPING UP WITH WRITING PROGRESS

As I meet with each student, I jot down my observations of the child's writing behaviors on an Independent Writing observation sheet (see reproducible on page 145). On the bottom of each sheet, I record any patterns I notice.

Reviewing this sheet helps me determine which skill and strategy mini-lessons I need to teach. And checking the sheet every day before Independent Writing reminds me which children I still need to meet with.

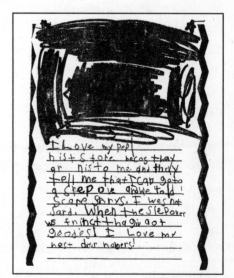

Independent-Writing Records

Student's Name	Date	Observations
Vanessa	3/7	Worked on Adding More Information to Story
Jonathan	3/7	Prompted to problem solve the word (man) by using known word (can)
Andre	3/7	Prompted to articulate word slowly and record sounds. (Used Alphabet Chart)
Diamond	3/7	Prompted to Reread text and cross out a word that didn't make sense or sound right.
Michael	3/7	Sticking to one topic and adding more detail to the topic.

Patterns Noticed and Ideas for Mini-Lessons:

- Spelling Strategies - Articulating Words slowly Using Known word to get to a new word.

- Adding More Information to Story

- Rereading Text and checking to see if it makes sense and sounds right.

A VARIETY OF GENRES

Throughout the year, I make sure children have a chance to discover that various genres require different styles of writing and to try out different styles of writing themselves. Here are some of the kinds of writing we work on—either in journals or on special format sheets.

❋ Personal Narratives

At the beginning of the year children use blank journals to describe a single event in their own lives. They might write about an event on the playground or what they had for lunch. It's up to them to choose what they want to write about. Later in the year, they write stories that include several events that are linked—maybe a few things that happened during a school day. I model my own stories (see pages

▲ I love my people next door because they are nice to me and they tell me that I can go to a sleepover and we told scary stories. I was not scared. When the sleepover was finished they gave out goodies. I love my next-door neighbors!

116–121 for an example) and read aloud a variety of literature that describes common personal experiences that they, too, can write about. (See "Books That Promote Personal Connections" on the Great Read Alouds for Kindergarten list, pages 95–96.)

❋ Labeling and List Books

Labeling books show one word and a picture of the word per page. To prepare children to write their own, I read a variety of labeling books aloud and demonstrate how to write one on a chart tablet.

Before I write, I think aloud to demonstrate for children how I choose my topic and decide on the things I want to include in my book. For example, if my topic is *My Classroom*, I tell children that I want to include the words *books, children, crayons, calendar,* and *word wall*. I write the title and author on

> ### A Few Good Labeling Books
>
> *At Home* by Sian Tucker (Simon & Schuster)
> *Baby's ABC* by Steve Shevett and Anita Shevett (Random House, 1986)
> *Baby's First Words* by Lars Wik (Random House, 1985)
> *Let's Go* by Sian Tucker (Simon & Schuster, 1993)

the first page, and then on the next page, I draw a picture for one of the words and write the word under it. I do the same thing for each word. I also think aloud about ways that I can end the labeling book, referring to labeling books we've read together to get ideas. This occurs over the course of a week, taking one step at a time.

I provide children with little blank books (pieces of paper stapled together) to use to write their own labeling books. The students choose their own topics, and as I hand out the blank books, they tell me the topic they have chosen and what words they'll use. This helps children focus on their idea and helps me assess their ability to conceptualize and follow through with consistency. Topic ideas are limitless—food, fruits, things in school, animals, family, and so on. This is a great activity to do at the beginning of the year, when children are learning how to focus on, and write about, one topic. It also helps them gain practice in slowly articulating words and recording the sounds they hear.

▲ *Class labeling book display from MaryAnn Wainstock's class*

You can take this concept a step further and have children write list books that have a repetitive pattern, such as *I like _____ , I am _____ , I can _____ , My Dad is _____ ,* and that include a wider range of ideas and words. These labeling and list books are similar to the books children are reading at this level. They also introduce the notion of writing an ending to a book or story and writing about one topic. Labeling and list books are a good way to warm children up for writing personal narratives.

❋ How-To Pieces

Students enjoy writing how-to pieces that describe step-by-step completion of a familiar task. To introduce the concept of how-to pieces, I read aloud a variety of books written in this format.

How-To Books to Read Aloud

Fruit Salad by Andrea Butler (Literacy, 2000)

How to Make Salsa by Jaime Lucero (Mondo, 1996)

How to Make a Sandwich by Peter and Sheryl Sloan

The Laundromat by Jillian Cutting (Wright Group, 1996)

The Monster Sandwich by Joy Cowley (Wright Group, 1990)

Victor Makes a TV (Scott Foresman and Co., 1976)

As we discuss the features in the books, children notice that there's a how-to title, that the steps are numbered, that each step explains something to do, that there's a catchy ending, and that the pictures match the words.

I prepare special one-sheet page for how-to writing. I leave a line for the title at the top of the page, numbers and four lines for however many steps there are. I put an illustration box next to each numbered step. The children can also write the steps on one page and create their illustration on a separate page.

How-to Piece

Name _____ Date _____
Title: _____

1. _____
   _____
   _____
   _____

2. _____
   _____
   _____
   _____

3. _____
   _____
   _____
   _____

You'll want to format the how-to paper in a way you feel best suits the needs of your students. You may want to create separate numbered boxes with lines in them or make books with a page for each step. After I model the how-to process, the children create their own pieces over several days—one day for the title and one day for each step.

I start modeling how-to articles by choosing a title for my piece, let's say, *How to Make Peanut Butter Crackers.* I write that on the title line. Then I give the children their paper and ask them to choose a how-to title for an activity that they know a lot about and feel they could teach to someone else. They tell me their titles before they write them on their papers, and I make a class list of all the topics. Examples have included:

◆ *How to Walk the Dog*   ◆ *How to Swim*

After the children and I come together to discuss the titles and revise them if necessary, each child writes his or her title on the title line, and I collect their papers.

The next day, I begin modeling how to create my *How to Make Peanut Butter Crackers* piece. I bring in the actual tools and ingredients for making the crackers because I want the children to see me saying and following the steps as I write them. The dialogue might go like this:

Ms. Franzese: *What should I write for the first step?*

Mark: *Put the peanut butter on the cracker.*

(I take the jar of peanut butter and put it on top of the cracker. The children laugh.)

Luis: *That's not right. You have to open the jar of peanut butter.*

Ms. Franzese: *(I say and write)* Open the jar of peanut butter. *What would be next?*

Shannon: *Pick up the knife.*

This kind of exchange shows the children how detailed they have to be in deciding on their steps.

At this point, I have children decide on the first step they're going to write for their topic and tell it to a partner. As the child verbalizes the step, the partner makes movements that match the description. This acting out helps children make sure that their step is clear and make changes if it's not. I have children tell me their first step before I return their papers so they can write it. I make any necessary suggestions, and then children write their first step independently.

Each day I demonstrate the next step needed to make a peanut butter cracker and follow the same routine as with the first step. Before I write any new steps, I model rereading to check and see if the text makes sense and sounds right. And of course, I model all the techniques I've been teaching the children in our other reading and writing lessons—leaving spaces, articulating words slowly,

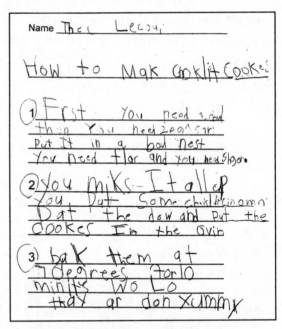

▲ How to Make Chocolate Cookies
1. First you need a bowl. Then you need 2 eggs and put it in a bowl. Next you need flour and you need sugar.
2. You mix it all up. You put some chocolate cinnamon. Pat the dough and put the cookies in the oven.
3. Bake them at 7 degrees for 10 minutes. Voila they are done. Yummy.

using punctuation marks at the end of a sentence, chunking, and matching pictures with the text. When I finish my how-to, we discuss catchy ways to end it, and the children go back and add endings to their own pieces.

✳ Nonfiction Writing

Composing pieces that share information about topics the children are studying is a great way to practice writing skills and reinforce learning. MaryAnn Wainstock had her kindergarten students study the life cycle of a butterfly and then record their observations. Tracy Markowitz did something different. She taught about snails, and her students wrote fact sheets.

I had children work with partners to write letters to people in our school—the principal, a cafeteria worker, the janitor, other teachers, and so on—asking for information about their jobs. They thought of questions they wanted to ask their assigned staffer, and I provided paper formatted for a personal letter. After I modeled the procedure, the children wrote and sent their letters. They received great responses and were excited about reading these to the class.

Informational Writing Format

> Facts about Snails
>
> Snails hid in rooks
>
> if periwinkle do not hal on to rooks Thy Wont Liv
>
> Some Snails have eyes Some dat The ones in the land have eyes But Thernes in the def se dat

▲ **Facts-About sheet**
Facts about snails
Snails hide in rocks.
If periwinkles do not hold onto rocks they won't live. Some snails have eyes. Some don't. The ones in the land have eyes but the ones in the deep sand don't.

There's no limit to the informational topics your students might write about. And creating formats such as the personal letter, the how-to paper, and the Facts-About sheet to provide structure helps young children focus on their task.

✳ Literature Responses

Responding to literature is also a critically important part of building literacy—especially since it underscores the child's connection to a text. Writing responses to literature helps make that connection concrete. In my class, students write retellings of stories I've read aloud or covered in Shared Reading. The children are prepared to retell stories in writing by their Read-Aloud experiences throughout the year where they retell the story aloud, make personal connections, and discuss their favorite parts.

To model a written retelling, I choose a familiar Big Book with a simple story line. Then after I have children verbally retell the beginning of the story, I provide each child with three blank sheets of paper. I draw some lines for writing and leave a blank space for a picture. On the first sheet, I model writing the beginning of the story, and

children write their own version of the beginning of the story on their first sheets. During the following two days, we use the other two sheets to write the middle and ending of the story. I explain and model how to use such words as *first, then, next,* and *finally,* for a retelling.

After children complete all three parts, they put the story together in correct sequential order. When they've gained enough practice writing retellings, they are ready to retell the whole story without breaking it into parts.

Students also write about their favorite parts of the story and text-to-self connections, which they've become familiar with from Read-Aloud and Guided Reading experiences.

Response to Literature

> One day the poor man and his wife got a goose. The goose laid a golden egg. They were happy and rich. They wanted more golden eggs. They cut the goose to look for more gold. The goose died and they 3/20/00 were poor.

▲ **Retelling** (The Goose That Laid the Golden Egg)
One day the poor man and his wife got a goose. The goose laid a golden egg. They were happy and rich. They wanted more golden eggs. They cut the goose to look for more gold. The goose died and they were poor.

❈ Poetry

Children do enjoy poetry. I read a variety of poems to children, and we discuss their various features. I choose poems that have beat and rhythm, poems with descriptive words, list poems, narrative poems, poems that start and end the same way, poems with repetitive lines, and simile poems in which things are compared. We talk about what they notice about each poem and look at how poems' words are written on the page very differently than the way words in story form are written. We discuss the poets' choice of topics and notice that they write about feelings, specific things and places, memories, and anything that may have been important to them.

Regie Routman has gathered a wonderful collection of poems written by kindergartners in *Kid's Poems: Teaching Kindergarteners to Love Writing Poetry* (Scholastic, 2000). Children love to hear and discuss these poems written by their peers, and they inspire children to write their own poems using similar features and topics.

I start each poetry Independent Writing session by reading a couple of poems that have similar features, and then students and I compose a poem using that feature. For example, I may read some rhythmic list poems in which ideas are listed around similar thematic topics (these often begin and end the same way). Then we write our own rhythmic list poem. Children are actively involved in the process and offer many suggestions for topics. Before writing each new line, I model going back to the beginning of the poem, rereading it, and seeing if the new line sounds right. Here's a list poem one class wrote about school:

School
Children Learning
Teachers Teaching
Principals Smiling
Custodians Cleaning
School

Now children write their own rhythmic list poems. Notice how they applied the techniques that were demonstrated to them. As they write, I may select a poem that a student is working on and use it as a teaching tool for the other students.

> cor t os
> I lIKe
> DonlDuK
> cartons
> I lIKe
> Bugs Bonny
> cartons
> I like
> TweTy BerD
> cartons cartoscartes

> BooKs
> Big books
> liddl books
> skiny Books
> esy books
> hard books
> thats all.

▲ *Repetitive use of the word* **cartoon:**
Cartoons
I like
Donald Duck
Cartoons
I Like
Bugs Bunny
Cartoons
I like Tweety Bird
Cartoons, cartoons, cartoons

▲ *Catchy ending:*
Books
Big books
Little books
Skinny books
Easy books
Hard books
That's all.

PUBLISHING

Kindergartners' published writing needs to meet certain standards, but less stringent ones than those appropriate for the higher grades. At first the pieces simply need to make sense, stay on one topic, and include pictures that match the words. Later on, children start to include titles, endings, and more information.

I have children select a piece of writing to publish from their varied Independent Writing experiences. They use the original pieces as they wrote them—without rewriting. I want writing to be—and remain—a joyful experience. I don't correct spelling errors on these pieces, but I have children correct any misspelled quick-and-easy words that they can see on the word wall. If a piece of writing is especially hard to read, I use conventional spelling to rewrite it on a sticky note and stick the note on the bottom of the child's piece. Sometimes we throw "publishing parties," where children read their stories and poems to parents and friends. Copies of the work can be laminated and compiled into a book for display. Before the party, children practice reading their pieces aloud clearly and with expression. The publishing parties are exciting and fun and further empower children as readers and writers.

▲ *Publishing display from MaryAnn Wainstock's classroom*

THROUGHOUT-THE-YEAR WRITING SAMPLES

Here are some samples of two children's writing from the beginning to the end of the year. I'm convinced that the key to the great progress the children made is the combination of constant modeling, writing every day, and learning from each other's pieces.

Gonzalo

▲ I saw balloons.

▲ I couldn't eat by myself. Now I can.

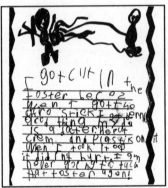

▲ I got cut in the toaster because when I got the churro stick I got burned. Good thing my dad is a doctor. He put cream and plastic on it. When I took it off it didn't hurt. I am never going to touch that toaster again!

Sylvia

▲ I like to go to the park.

▲ I am an Italian. I like to eat pasta and zucchini. I speak Italian. I say Cia Papa Io te voi bene. I love you. I am going to Italy for my papa's birthday. I get so many kisses in Italy. I love being Italian! Ciao!

▲ How to swim in a little pool.

You put a bathing suit on. Then you go to the pool. You jump in the water.

You move your hands and kick your feet. You go out of the pool.

You change your bathing suit and lay down in the sun. You should go swimming.

Independent Writing Records

Student's Name	Date	Observations

Patterns Noticed and Ideas for Mini-Lessons:

Chapter Nine

Word Study:
At the Heart of Literacy

Word Study teaches children about the way letters and words look and what they sound like. Children use word-study techniques to take words apart for understanding when they're reading and put words together to create meaning when they're writing. And with lots of Word Study practice, these techniques become automatic. As you have seen in this book, Word Study is integrated throughout a balanced literacy program.

WORD STUDY IN CONTEXT

Shared Reading (Chapter Two) teaches children about the features of letters and words and what letters and words sound like. Children gain an increasing

bank of high-frequency words and learn to manage letter clusters, blends, digraphs, and chunks when reading and writing. They begin to understand that a word they know can help them figure out one they don't. And they practice using visual cues (what the word looks like) to figure out words. Reading nursery rhymes, poems, and songs with the whole class develops their ability to identify words that sound the same. Children begin to notice that most of the time words that sound the same have the same chunk, and they learn to problem-solve new words using this information.

Reading Play Stations (Chapter Three) actively engage students in a variety of letter and word activities they've been exposed to in Shared Reading.

Guided Reading (Chapter Four) gives students the opportunity to apply their newly-acquired knowledge—to problem-solve and gain meaning from text by using what they know about letters and words.

Read-Aloud (Chapter Five) introduces students to new vocabulary and uses the context of a story to problem-solve meanings of new words.

Independent Reading (Chapter Six) gives students the opportunity to apply word-study skills, such as looking for known parts and chunks in words, recognizing high-frequency words within context as opposed to in isolation, letter-sound correspondence, one-to-one matching and other basic concepts about print on their own.

Interactive and Shared Writing (Chapter Seven) model using problem-solving strategies and word-study skills to form and write new words.

Independent Writing (Chapter Eight) requires children to apply all that they know about letters and words to construct their own meaningful text.

In their book *Word Matters*, Gay Su Pinnell and Irene Fountas list word-study benchmarks (see right) that kindergarten students should achieve by the end of the

Word Study Skills Kindergartners Should Master

By the end of the year, kindergartners should be able to . . .

* understand concepts about print.

* distinguish between letters and words.

* understand that words are made up of letters.

* write most letters in the correct direction and standard form.

* differentiate between upper- and lower-case letters.

* name and locate letters in different positions in words.

* articulate words slowly.

* hear and identify sounds in words, especially rhymes, syllables, and initial and final consonants.

* know most letter-sound associations for consonants and easy-to-hear vowel sounds.

* recognize their own names and the names of classmates.

* write and read these twenty-five high-frequency words: *a, at, an, and, am, can, do, go, he, in, I, is, it, like, me, my, no, see, she, so, the, to, up, we, Child's name*.

* make new words with the same rime or chunk, such as *can, man, tan*.

From *Word Matters: Teaching Phonics and Spelling in the Reading/Writing* Classroom by Gay Su Pinnell and Irene Fountas, Heinemann, 1998

school year. I keep these benchmarks in mind as I evaluate my students, and I've found that by following the literacy program I've laid out, the students master these benchmarks and much more. They can usually read and write many more high-frequency words and are aware of several blends, digraphs, letter clusters, and chunks.

WORD STUDY ACTIVITIES

Word-study information can be divided in to three categories: how letters and words look (visual), how they sound (phonological), and the relationships between them. My teaching goal is to create learning experiences and activities that translate this information into skills that children can apply automatically to their reading and writing. The three aspects of word study and the skills that match them are integrated throughout the previous chapters on reading and writing. You'll want to be sure you've built them into your literacy program.

Word-Study Skills

VISUAL

The ability to . . .

* distinguish features of letters (slants, sticks, tunnels, circles, dots)
* recognize and form letters
* differentiate between letters and words
* identify letters within words
* recognize letter clusters, including digraphs, blends, and chunks
* be familiar with shape and length of words
* recognize high-frequency words

PHONOLOGICAL

The ability to . . .

* recognize that letters are comprised of sound
* recognize that words are comprised of sequences of sound
* identify similar sounds in words
* differentiate between beginning, middle, and ending sounds of words
* identify various sounds of digraphs, blends, and chunks
* listen for rhythms, parts, and syllables of words

GRAPHOPHONIC

The ability to . . .

* match sounds to letters
* identify and match patterns of sounds to parts of words
* apply visual and phonological knowledge of digraphs, blends, and chunks to problem-solve new words

The following word-study activities are manageable for kindergartners, include all three types of skills, and are fun, playful ways for the children to build skills.

✸ Learning the Letters

▲ *Students practice saying letter names.*

Every day at the beginning of the year, before I introduce a Shared Reading book or poem, I place up to eight magnetic letters (not in alphabetic sequence) in a straight line across the top of a magnetic board. I pull down a series of letters to the middle of the board and have the children say their names as I pull them down. One series might be *C, D, c, E, D, d, e,* and *c.* The letters are out of sequence so that children learn how identify them out of the context of the alphabetic sequence.

After children state the names of all the letters, I ask one child to come to the board and sort the letters according to upper- and lower-case. I also ask students to pull down letters from the series according to their distinct features. For example, if the series is *L, l, N, m, M,* and *n.* I might say "Pull down the letters with tunnels" or "Pull down the letters with a slanted and straight stick." I also have the children pull down the letter that corresponds to the specific picture icon on the alphabet chart that we recite each day. For example, I might say "Pull down the letter that *dog* begins with." As one child pulls down the letters, another writes them on a wipe-off board. I spend two to three days working on the same series until I feel students have mastered each of those letters. The approximately five minutes this activity takes is time well spent. It's such an effective way to develop visual awareness, I include it as a Reading Play Station activity (see Chapter Three).

✸ Using Name Games to Teach Letters and Sounds

In her book, *Phonics They Use,* Patricia Cunningham points out that children who enter school without any reading or writing skills will "develop those abilities and concepts essential for success" by participating in literacy activities that incorporate their names. Most kindergartners come to school knowing their names and love focusing on them. By using the written words that children are most familiar with (their names) as a foundation, they become more aware of specific letter sounds, features, and spelling patterns. At the beginning of the year, after introducing each child's name as a word-study activity, I put them on our Word Wall, which stays up

all year for children to refer to. At the same time, I also write each child's name on construction paper and have children trace over their names or glue on macaroni, buttons, Cheerios, and so on. I hang these around the classroom.
Here are some other name activities you can use:

Power Names. Each day before Shared Reading, I make a child's name—we call them *power names*—with magnetic letters and present it to the class. The child whose name is on the board comes up and uses more letters to remake the name. Once the letters are in place, I ask the child to count them and state the names of each letter. As a class, we clap the syllable beat of the name as we say it out loud. We also discuss the first and last letters of the name, as well as the similarities and differences between that child's name and the names of others in the class.

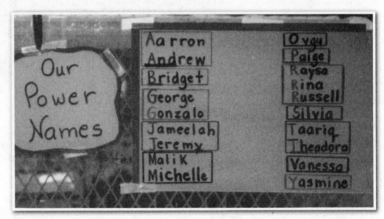

▲ *Children learn sounds and spelling from their names in MaryAnn Wainstock's class.*

I also use the children's power names to help them learn specific sounds and spelling patterns formed by the letters in them. For example, we discussed the *sh* and *ch* sounds in Shantel's and Richard's names and the *th* sound in Jonathan's name. The children also learn from the names *Cirena* and *Cathy* that the *c* sometimes makes the *s* sound like in *celery* or the *k* sound like in *cat*. Other examples include the *ing* in Irving's name, the *Qu* in Quinn's, the /ee/ sound of *y* in Kelly's name, and the /er/ sound from Amber's name. After we talk about the sounds in the names we're discussing, I write them on a class-name chart and highlight the specific part we discussed. I use this chart as a reference tool for teaching writing and reading skills.

The children apply all of the knowledge they accumulate from examining their names to reading and writing other words. For example, when they want to read or write a word such as *shake*, the children might say, *It's like the* sh *in Shantel's name!* And they'll see that the *y* at the end of *baby* makes the /ee/ sound like in *Kelly*. After you have gone through all of the first names in your class, start using the children's last names as a learning tool. Students also practice their letters and sounds in the name-game Reading Play Stations (see Chapter Three).

Sign-In Practice. Each day when children arrive at the classroom, they write their names on a sign-in sheet. In our room, children sit four to a table, and I put a folder with a sign-in sheet at every table. At the beginning of the year, I list each child's

names on the sheet as a model, and they copy their name. Later in the year, the children are able to sign in without the model, and I leave it off.

Environmental Print Names. (Adapted from *Jumpstarters* by Aldridge, Kirkland, and Kuby.) At the beginning of the year, I ask children to bring in some printed text that represents something they like to eat and that begins with the same

▲ *Environmental print names from Katherine Schneid's room*

letter as their first name. For example, Susan might bring in a Snickers candy wrapper, or Michael might bring in the McDonald's logo. I take pictures of the children and mount the piece of environmental print next to their pictures. For each, I write a caption that includes the child's name, the word *likes*, and the word for the environmental print. Examples include: *Tommy likes Tootsie Rolls* and *Frank likes Frosted-Flakes*. I post these *I like* photos on an environmental print board. Of course, children can bring in environmental print on a host of topics other than food.

✷ Alphabet Charts

I place a large alphabet chart by the meeting area where we have Shared and Interactive Writing.

Students read the alphabet chart during Shared Reading every day. I point to the capital and lower-case letters as well as the corresponding pictures. The children say the name of the letters and then the name of the picture. For example, *A, a, Apple; C, c, cat; F, f, Fish!* This technique, described by Dorn, French and Jones in *Apprenticeship in Literacy*, allows for quick letter recognition and sound correspondence. Once your students have had enough practice reciting the chart, take it a step further by using a sticky note to mask some of the letters or a picture.

◆ Cover the beginning, middle, or ending letters in a series of three letters and ask the children to figure out what letter is missing. This prepares students for the *Missing Letter* Reading Play Station game (Chapter Three).

◆ Cover a picture on the chart and have the students tell you what picture is covered based on its letter.

◆ Cover some of the letters, and have the students tell you what letters correspond to the pictures.

Once children have mastered the alphabet chart, they can begin on another chart that contain blends and the digraphs *sh, th, wh,* and *ch.* We work on the digraphs chart first and then move on from there. They recite these charts the same way they did the alphabet chart. I make sure that the pictures associated with the blends and digraphs represent things children know. So, if a child is confronted with the word *this,* he can recognize the *th* word part by associating it with the word *thumb* that's on the chart. It's amazing to see how quickly children learn blends and digraphs by simply reading and referring to these charts. I frequently refer to them when I write with the children. I make mini versions of the charts for the children to use when they're writing independently (see Chapter Eight).

❋ Letter Formation

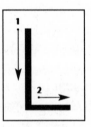

It's important to describe the sequence of how letters are formed when you're teaching children to write them. As the children practice writing letters, have them say aloud how they're moving their pencil. For example, if they're making the letter *L,* they would say "down and across" while forming the letter. I use the Zaner-Bloser Alphabet as a reference for forming letters.

❋ Alphabet Book

Children and I enjoy making a class alphabet book. We give each letter two pages in a blank Big Book or large chart tablet. One page is for a story I create based on cut-out pictures that represent the specific letter sound I'm introducing. First I tell the story and then write it as a Shared Writing experience. The other page is for words and pictures the children come up with for the same letter sound.

For example, if we were working on the letter *Bb,* I might cut out pictures of balloons, a bear, books, biscuits, and a girl (I'd name Betty). I'd tell the story: *It was Betty's birthday. She got balloons, books, and a teddy bear for her birthday. She ate biscuits at her party.* Then I ask the children what they noticed about the pictures and what they heard in the story. They discover what letter we're studying by noticing the similar letter-sound correspondence represented by the pictures. Next, children are called upon to retell the story, taking turns looking at the pictures and reciting its parts. As they tell the story, I write the words on the alphabet book page and stick the pictures next to the appropriate lines of text. After I write down the story, I have children locate the letter we're focusing on within it. Students then draw their own pictures to represent that letter. Children say the words that correspond to the pictures slowly and record the sounds they hear. Each child's picture goes in the

class alphabet book with the appropriate letter.

I like to take photographs of all the children and put each child's photo on the first page of the letter his or her name begins with. The students read this book the same way they read the Alphabet Chart (*Bb balloon, Bb bike*). A picture associated with the letter helps children to recall the name and sound of the letter. And they enjoy referring to the alphabet book stories and reading them throughout the year.

❋ Learning About Chunks

I begin the year by immersing children in rhyming poems, especially nursery rhymes. I want them to practice hearing and saying words that sound the same so that they can understand the concept of chunking, also referred to as *onset and rime*. I explain to children that the reason these words sound the same is because they have the same *chunk*. We frame individual words in the poems and highlight their chunks. As children read poems throughout the year, I continue having them locate the rhyming words and their chunks. They use what they know about familiar parts of words to figure out new words that contain the same chunks. This concept is also referred to as *analogy*. It's important for children to acquire an increasing bank of quick-and-easy (high-frequency) words, so they can apply their knowledge of the chunks in the words they know to figuring out new words.

▲ *Chunk Charts from MaryAnn Wainstock's classroom*

I make and post separate charts to illustrate the new chunks the children are learning. These charts serve as references during reading and writing sessions. For example, if we were working on the word *went*, I chart the words *went, tent, sent*. The first letters (or part) of the words (*w, t,* and *s*) are written in one color and the chunk (*ent*) in another. I list three or four words for each new chunk. I hang the small charts along a string in the meeting area or post them in an easily accessible area. I like to put them in the meeting area because that's where I do most of my teaching and modeling. As each new chunk is introduced, I add it to the word-study activities in the Reading Play Stations (see Chapter Three).

Take a look at Patricia Cunningham's *Phonics They Use* for more chunking activities that work well in the kindergarten classroom.

CLASSROOM WORD WALLS

❋ Make-Up of the Word Wall

You can put your Word Wall on chart paper, a magnetic board, or any surface where you can display words so that they are easily reachable, removable and on eye level with the children. I place the words in alphabetical order under letter cards, each of which includes an upper- and lower-case letter and the same picture that represents that letter on our class alphabet chart. I write the word wall words on index cards, and make them removable so children can have access to them when they're reading and writing. If the word wall is a magnetic board, put magnetic tape on the back of each word or use Velcro® to attach the words to a different type of surface. I cut out the words in the shape of their configuration to exaggerate the visual features of each letter in the word and the word as a whole.

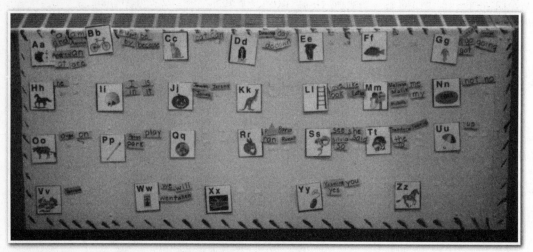

▲ *Word Wall from MaryAnn Wainstock's class*

❋ Adding Words to the Wall

I post a quick-and-easy word on the Word Wall after I've introduced it during Shared Reading. But first I have children form the word with magnetic letters, write it on a wipe-off board, and locate it within the context of the story. The students tell me which letter to place the word under. I use Patricia Cunningham's term *star words* from *Phonics They Use* to describe words that students will be able to use to make new words. For example, *got* is a star word because if you know *got*, you can get to

not, hot, and *spot*. I put a star sticker next to the word on the index card before I put it on the word wall. Once the students have mastered the star word, I demonstrate how to make a new word from the known word.

Word Wall Games

Word Wall games help children gain fluency with visual sources of information so that they can process high-frequency words automatically as they read and write. Before Interactive Writing (Chapter Seven), I play word games with the children.

- ***Starts Like, Sounds Like.*** (From Patricia Cunningham and Richard Allington's book *Classrooms That Work*, 1999) Every child has his or her own wipe-off board and marker. I say, "I'm thinking of a word and it is on the word wall. It starts like *window* (I refer to the window picture icon from the alphabet chart) and sounds like *tent*." The children write the word *went* on their boards, and we check it as a class. I may then take it a step further and ask children to look at the word on their wipe-off boards and write another word that has the same chunk (such as *tent*). I'll say a sentence including that word: "When I went camping, I slept in a *tent*." Other examples include "The word is on the word wall. It starts like *ladder* and it sounds like *bike* . . . (*like*)" "It starts like *wheel* and makes sense in the sentence *I like _____ we go to the movies* . . . (*when*)" "It starts like *mailbox*, sounds like *by* and makes sense in the sentence _____ *Mom loves me so much!* . . . (*My*)."

- ***Hangman.*** We also play a game similar to hangman. I make the shape of the word in boxes for each letter and then say a sentence with a blank for the word. For example, *I _____ a toy for my birthday (got).*" The children tell me what letters would fit into the shape of the boxes.

  As the children give me letters, we check to see if the word they guessed would make sense in the sentence.

- ***Look-Say-Name-Cover-Write-Check***. Using this technique developed by Diane Snowball (*Spelling K- 8: Planning and Teaching*), I write a word on the large wipe off board and tell the children to look at the word, say it, and name the letters. Then I cover the word, and children write it on their small wipe-off boards. I uncover the word and they place a checkmark next to the word on their boards if it is correctly spelled.

Personal Dictionaries

Using blank writing paper and binders, I make a personal dictionary for every child in the classroom. Dorn, French & Jones also discuss this technique in *Apprenticeship in Literacy*. Each letter has its own page with the same letter and picture icons from

our large classroom alphabet chart. Every Friday the children update their personal dictionaries. They add the quick-and-easy words that we worked on during the week.

We review the new words as a whole class. Children, working in groups of three, form the words using sets of index cards with the letters (one to a card) written on them. The cards contain only the letters of the words for that particular session. For example, if we're forming the new words *like* and *it,* each group will have letter cards for *l, i, k, e, t.*

Before we discuss each word, I model the procedure. I ask one child to come up and locate the new word in the text we've been reading that week. Then I make the word on a magnetic board or the overhead projector so the whole class can see. Next I ask children to do the same using their letter cards. The children work together, sort through the letters on the cards, and form the new words they are learning. Each child in the group of three gets a chance to make the word with the cards.

Finally children then write the new word in their personal dictionaries. For each word, I ask children whether the word belongs at the beginning, middle, or end of the alphabet.

Do you hear what I hear? I do this activity to give children practice with articulating words slowly and writing the sounds they hear accurately. Each morning as the children are settling in, I show them a picture of a familiar item. The word for the item must have distinct sounds and contain sounds of specific chunks, digraphs, and blends that I want children to practice. For example, I show them a picture of a bed that I've tacked onto the chart tablet. Children identify the picture and articulate the word *bed* slowly. Then they take turns trying to write the word based on the sounds they hear as they say the word again. I remind them to refer to the alphabet chart to support their letter-sound correspondence. We look at all of the children's versions of the word, and I show the correct spelling. We discuss the different parts of the word. You can then keep these pictures in a class "labeling book" (see page 138) that highlights the familiar sounds, parts, and chunks in the words you discussed. Children can use the book as a dictionary of sounds that they can refer to when they're writing.

SPELLING STARTERS

❁ Buddy Spell Checks

(Idea from Fountas and Pinnell in *Word Matters*)

Each week I have students pair off to practice spelling the new words we learned that week during reading and writing activities. I make up a master sheet that lists the

new words. The partners take turns leading each other. One child reads the words and the other writes them in a spelling notebook. Make the notebook by stapling together a few pieces of paper with three numbered horizontal lines (one for each new word). Keep the spelling notebooks together in a basket or separately in each child's cubby. Once the partners have both written the words, they check with the master list to see if they spelled them correctly. They cross out any misspelled word and rewrite the word correctly next to it. Later when they're at the *Look-Say-Name-Cover-Write-Check* Reading Play Station, they go to their spell-check notebook and practice the word they misspelled using the technique from the station. I can periodically look at their notebooks and assess how they are doing with specific words, skills, or self-correcting behaviors.

✸ Spelling Strategies

Here's a list of strategies that I teach my students to use when they're trying to figure out how to write a word they don't know:

◆ Say the word slowly and write the letters that go with the sounds they hear.

◆ Check to see if the word looks right. (If a child tells me how to spell a word, I'll write it as they tell me, even if it's incorrect. But I'll ask . . . "Does it look right?" I want them to develop a sense of when a word looks right and when it doesn't. If the spelling is incorrect, I provide the correct spelling immediately.)

◆ Use the aids we have in the classroom—the word wall, personal dictionary, the alphabet charts, and the chunk, blend, and digraph charts.

◆ Break the word into smaller parts and write the parts of the word they know.

◆ Think about words that sound alike.

◆ Look for chunks in words. Use what they know to figure out new words.

◆ Look for words around the classroom that can help them.

◆ Remember the way a word looks from reading.

Adapted from *Word Matters* by Irene Fountas and Gay Su Pinnell (Heinemann, 1998)

ASSESSING WORD-STUDY SKILLS

I get ideas for Word Study lessons by assessing my students' knowledge of letters, sounds, and words within the context of reading and writing. When I analyze running records and writing samples, I look for the strengths and weaknesses that a student demonstrates in using visual, phonological, and graphophonic information.

Shown below are examples of writing samples and how they informed my teaching.

The *ay* chunk

▲ *This sample, which was done after I taught the ay chunk, shows that the child transferred what she learned to her writing.*

The word *like*

▲ *I noticed that the author of this sentence didn't know how to write the word like. Since like is a quick-and-easy word that I use often in my lessons, I made a mental note to reinforce it.*

Word-Study Skills Teach Kindergartners to . . .

- ✴ articulate words slowly and record the appropriate letter sound in writing.
- ✴ practice reading and writing high-frequency words.
- ✴ be aware of and use letter clusters, digraphs, and blends such as *sh, ch, wh, th*.
- ✴ understand that some letters have two different pronunciations: *cat, circus, excited*.
- ✴ add *s* to words to make them plural.
- ✴ add *ing* and *ed* to base words.
- ✴ be aware that *y* at the end of a word can be represented by the long /e/ or /i/ sound, as in *happy* and *my*.
- ✴ be aware that there is a silent e at the end of some words.
- ✴ be aware of the *er* sound.
- ✴ use analogy to write new words.
- ✴ know the following chunks *all, ake, an, at, ay, en, et, ent, ill, in, ing, it, ike, ot ,op, ow, ook, ome, go-no-so, my-by-try, he-she-be*.
- ✴ reread to clarify confusions.
- ✴ check to see if everything looks right, makes sense, and sounds right.

Word Study occurs during all reading and writing activities. I often use word study games as a playful interlude to help with classroom transitions. I may line children up by asking them to stand up if their name begins with the same letter as *tiger*. I may recite a familiar nursery rhyme and leave out a word for children to fill in while we are waiting to go into the cafeteria. Children enjoy these activities, which reinforce their learning.